# BRENDA S. TURNER

# MISSING PIECES

## THE TRUTH

Brilliant Books Literary
137 Forest Park Lane Thomasville
North Carolina 27360 USA

Because of the dynamic nature of the Internet, any web addresses or links contained in this book may have changed since publication and may no longer be valid. The views expressed in this work are solely those of the author and do not necessarily reflect the views of the publisher, and the publisher hereby disclaims any responsibility for them.

ISBN: 979-8-88945-104-4 (paperback)
ISBN: 979-8-88945-106-8 (hardback)
eISBN: 979-8-88945-105-1

Printed in the United States of America

# MISSING PIECES: THE TRUTH

The last two days were very strange to me. I am in a battle that a lot of people would not understand. The glory of it is I am still standing strong in the Lord. There is no other way to understanding this life I have lived. Back in the early 1960s, I can remember going to a little white church named Oak Grove Methodist Church in a small city of Gordo, Alabama. Gordo is where my mother grew up. My grandmother, her dad and his dad dug wells for a living. It is so ironic that their last name is Wells.

Often, on Sunday mornings, my grandmother and grandfather would take us to that little white church. The bees would fly over our heads. The windows would be up, and we would all have fans fanning trying to stay cool. Every now and then, I could feel a breeze enter through the windows. We had cool water on the front porch with little white pointed paper cups. The amazing thing was I never saw anyone get stung by a bee. Every now and then, an older man we called Uncle Lonnie would swipe one with his fan as he began to pray. Every year in June, we would have homecoming at church and people would have their tables set with food as far as you could see. My Uncle Golden would be on the back of his truck with an old drink cooler. It was red with a Coke bottle on it. He would look down and smile at us and offer us a drink. He would push the lid back, and we would put our hands down into the cold ice and pulled up different flavors. We could see the color through the bottle. It was like fishing to the children.

That meant to come right back, but we could not resist. As I was running backward to slide again, I did not notice the big glass behind me. I hit the glass very hard, and kept running as fast as I could. I could hear my sister calling me, so I stopped. She looked down at my leg and told me that I was bleeding. When I saw my leg, I started to run again. I just wanted to get to my grandmother. I was so afraid! I was not worried that my leg was cut all the way to the bone. I was more afraid of getting in trouble for breaking the glass. My grandmother was so upset! The cut was so big! My thigh was open. It was so deep that they had to double stitch it on the inside and out. The principal came to my house to see about me. What a surprise that was for me because he gave me some money. I really knew everything was going to be all right. I learned later that as soon as I went through the window, the whole front window came crashing down. Now I can see grandmother and granddaddy's prayers being answered. I was only four years old at that time. I did not know at the time that prayer was awesome.

My mother and grandparents continued to teach us about the Almighty God. My soul is so weak, but our God will make a way. Everything that happened to me that was good, God did it, and now I can tell it. In my early days, I didn't know that I had someone with me through it all. At the time, I was a child washed in the blood of Jesus and did not know it at all. In spite of it all, Jesus is and always will be Jesus. There is no other way.

As the years went by, my grandmother grew sicker every year, but still growing stronger in the Lord. One Tuesday night, we went to a prayer meeting at my grandparents' home. I was about nine or ten years old. I witnessed my mother being touched by my grandmother and was filled with the spirit of God. During those days, I did not understand the power of God. I did not know that he was so powerful until my life continued. My grandmother did not stop praising the Lord until I was in the fifth grade. Early one morning, we were awakened and told to come to the phone; our mother needed to talk to us. She told us that our grandmother had passed on. What a nightmare! The lady that was my grandmother was gone? I felt so alone and afraid. I would see her in my dreams a lot. She was with me even when I went to the housing project to play. After dark, she would walk me home as a puff of white smoke shining in the darkness. She would go inside the house with me until I turned the lights on. That is when I knew, with no doubt, that she would always be with me.

My grandmother made sure we knew about the Lord. We had a choir stand sized to fit my aunt, my sister, about two more people, and me. My aunt taught my sister and me how to harmonize, and it would sound like a large choir singing. You could hear feet tapping the wooden floor to make music. Looking up at Uncle Golden's shining bright teeth made everything so bright.

Listening to the crackling sound of the rocks on the long dirt road was a peaceful sound. Looking out the window at all the plum trees along the side of the little narrow road made it impossible not to stop on the way in and in the way out sometimes.

Today is February 2, 2001. My grandfather is on my mind very strongly. I have come to realize that I miss him very much. Tears are flowing out of my eyes like a small stream. I can't control the tears, but I know they will soon stop. When we start morning worship, my grandfather would moan the old hymn  song that we would be singing. Every now and then, he would sing a few words; he would not miss a note. Every now and then, I would look over to my left. Granddaddy, we called him, would stand up and say, "Yes, Lord" and grand related. My grandmother's dad, his dad lived to be in his hundreds. The family lost count. Momma, we called her, would be praying. I believe just about everyone in the church lost count after about 106. I don't think anyone can remember his age. My grandmother's mother's sister, her daddy's sister, and first through fourth-generation cousins were all there. All praising to the Most High. Sometimes, there would be thunder and lightning, and we would keep praising the Lord. My mom made sure that we always went to church even after my grandmother passed on. My grandmother was a babysitter when my mom went to work. She took very good care of me. I could ask her questions all day, and she would answer all of them with meaning. She was powerful with God. I found that out as years went by. If I had a stomachache, she would rub my stomach and pray. She would cough up something and spit it out. The next thing I knew, I was feeling great and ready to go outside to play.

At that time, I did not know the things about God like I do now. My mother went to work in the summertime. My sister and I went to my grandmother's house. We played with some neighborhood friends that day. My grandmother came to the door and asked us to take my oldest brother some lunch to school. He cut grass for the school in the summertime. When we got there, we were amazed to see how shiny the floors were. We just had to run and slide on the floors. We were having so much fun, but we knew we were to do what my grandmother said.

I then became bitter at everyone that did not come to me in the right way all because I became immune to my grandmother not being around. At that time, I did not know that it was the correct way to feel, but not the proper way to react. My mom is the sweetest lady he would ever want to meet. She is so sweet. I never heard a curse word come out of her mouth. No matter what happened, she would always forgive anyone that would do her or her children wrong. She always thought us to forgive. I guess that is why I can't hold a grudge against anyone. I guess I picked it up somewhere along the way. I have forgiven over and over again. I do like what my mother taught me. I have learned over the years just to do the right thing and God will stand behind you through it all.

In my younger days, I was naïve, just like other children. Regardless of the obstacles that came along, I remembered what I was taught. Oh, how important that I knew that my grandmother taught my mother with her just as my mother taught her children. I grew up, over the years, with a grieving heart. I did not know that all the pain I was feeling was from the loss of my grandmother. I did not know that that was the problem at the time. I became more and more bitter over the years. I felt bitter against everyone. I felt cheated. No, grandmother and I did not know my father's mother because she passed on before I was born. Also, I have never seen a picture of her. My mind is racing trying to imagine her in my mind over the years. I met her sisters. When I look at them, I wonder, did she look like one of them? Now I can see myself through them. I know where I got the spunkiness from.

I knew I had to get self-control, but it was hard simply because I married at an early age. I was looking for something but did not know what I was looking for. I was seventeen years old and dating a guy who went into the U.S. Navy. He would call me when he came home for visits. After he got out of the Navy, we got married. I did not know that he became an alcoholic. He would drink all day until the ugliness would come out. He then began to beat me. It got worse every day. Poor me, I was trying to do what I was taught– to forgive and to respect our marriage vows till death do us part. It got harder every day. I had swollen eyes and heart for five years! I learned that he did not have self-control when he would drink all day. The most crucial moment was when he locked me the apartment for seven days and told me, on the seventh day, that he was going to kill me. I knew then that I was no longer dealing with him, but with the devil himself! I had to think and think fast. I don't feel back on what my mother and grandmother thought me more than ever. I had to believe it, claim it, and then receive it.

The first day, he had me take off all my clothes except my underclothes. He made me go into the living room, get on the floor, and pretend I was having sex with the devil! If I did not follow instructions, he would kick me everywhere until I did just what he said. I felt like a caged animal begging to be set free. The second day, he raped me all day long until I had no self-esteem.

He would knock me out a times. When I regained consciousness, I could see my bowel leavings all over the bed. No matter how hard I fought, he would not stop. The third day, he got hungry and began to eat. Every bowl he used he would hit me in the head, face, or anywhere that he could to hurt me. He would then laugh and remind me that he was going to kill me on the seventh day.

I knew I had to get with God above through the Almighty Jesus. I thought back on what my mother and grandmother told me. I began to pray to the Lord Almighty. The fourth day, he began to take the knife and swing it at me from time to time. He was so drunk. I was able to keep him from cutting me. He did not sleep for those seven days.

He just watched me even as I slept. The fifth day, he choked and hit me with anything he could find. We fought all day. I was so tired, but I kept praying and asking God to please give me strength to survive this. The sixth day, he was wide awake. He only trusted me to go to the bathroom. I could not understand why my downstairs neighbors did not help me or just call the police.

By now, I was alone, and no one could help me but God. I went in the bathroom and began to pray. I asked the Lord to help me. By now, my husband had about six locks on the front door so that I could not get out. I studied the locks every day as I walked by to and from the bathroom. The seventh arrived, and he told me he was ready to kill me. He had a bold devil working through him. He was bold enough to ask me if I was ready to die. I told him to let me use the bathroom first. I kept praying, "Lord, please help me!" What am I going to do? It came to my mind to just unlock the door and run. I said to myself, *How?* Something in my mind said to just unlock the door. I did not have a choice but to try or die. I opened the bathroom door. I could see him sitting on the side of the bed, smiling as he looked at the knife. I ran to the door and unlocked all six locks in a matter of seconds. All of them were different, but I got out. I ran to my neighbor's house. I was still in my underwear—what a shame, what a shame—but I was out! They opened the door looking surprised and sad. The lady of the house had a look of shame on her face, knowing that I knew that her husband beat on her also. By the way, we could hear each other fighting all the time. We lived in a duplex house. We lived upstairs, and we could hear everything that was said and done. She then gave me some clothes to put on. I asked for help, so she called her mother to come and get me. Her mother took me to her house, and I wore her daughter's clothes. The clothes and shoes were too big for me, but it did not matter.

It was winter in Cleveland, Ohio, with about four feet of snow. I was grateful for what these total strangers could do for me. They fed me and gave me money to buy personal needs. I felt a sense of freedom. I did not have relatives in this city other than my husband. This freedom went on about two weeks and one day, and it ended. We were sitting in their backyard barbecuing. I looked up and there he stood, the nightmare all over again. I was only nineteen years old and did not know much about the law back then, but I did know that they did not handle spouse abuse the way they do now. He then forced me to go back with him. When we got home, he apologized and promised not to hit me again. I knew, by now, that as soon as he had a drink, he was going to strike again. The knot grew larger in my stomach. The feeling was of deep fear that was always there regardless. No matter what I did for five long years, the fear stayed. I came to realize that no matter where I went, he would find me. At this realization, I lay across the bed to think. I thought about what my mother and family had taught me. I began to think of the vision I had of a man on Christmas Eve night.

A man was standing over me when I woke up about 2:00 a.m. He was tall and wore old clothes and an old hat. His beard was salt-and-pepper. His face was turned away from me, but I could see that his skin had a glow. It was the color of brass. Such beautiful skin. I felt a sense of peace just as I did that Christmas Eve night. At that moment, I knew that I had someone watching over me and that I was not alone. Whoever this man was, I could feel his presence from that moment on. I felt protected by someone that I could not see.

We later moved. When he would begin to hit me, something would happen. The lights would blow out and the television would still be playing, or the flowers in the house would begin to move. All kinds of unusual things would happen. I got stronger and was able to protect myself. I became less and less afraid of him. I fought back regardless. When he came to fight, I fought back until he left me alone.

I later moved from Detroit, back to Alabama, and then to Atlanta, Georgia. By now, I was exhausted and depressed. I was getting older and wiser. One day, it finally came to the point that it would be him or me. As I dressed for work one morning, he began to pick at me. He had been up all night drinking. By now, he was ready to fight, but that was his last draw. I got a knife, put him down in the chair, and put it around his neck. He was smiling. I believe he saw something in me to let him know that I was serious. I pressed the blade as hard as I could to the side of his neck. Actually, jail did not matter anymore. I had enough. Thank God for my sister, whom I rode to work with every morning. She came up to see what was taking me so long. She had a key to my apartment and I had one to hers. She and her husband came in and talked me out of killing him. The deal was to take him, along with a bottle of alcohol, to the Greyhound bus station. He was to never bother me again.

Though he was gone, I was left with fear, hate, and hurt. I then realized that I did not know who I was anymore. I was lost in a wide and cold world. My dearest mother would write me just about every day with encouraging words. My sister would come by to visit and take me out for rides. No matter what I did, I was still depressed. One day, I looked at myself in the mirror. I looked into my eyes and asked myself, "Who am I?" I thought back to when I was a little girl. I found myself and really focused on myself.

One morning, I did not know which way to turn. I was seeking for the answers to this puzzled life. I was led to a very dear friend's house. When I arrived, an older lady opened the door and asked me to come in. I felt a sense of peace the moment I walked inside. She welcomed me by inviting me to breakfast. My friend came from the back room, and they began to pray for me as if they knew I was in pain in my heart. After going to Sunday school, church, sunbeam meetings, prayer meetings at my grandparents' house every Tuesday night, community choir, church choir, and Bible study, it seemed as though I would have known all along what to do. The bitterness had gotten the best of me.

I slowly came around, but not like I should. I was looking at all men as the same. I even went as far as planning to kill him, and when I did try, God would, some way or another, prevent it. I really knew that he was for me and not against me because I could have gone to jail. My gun I had at the time clicked, instead of firing, and it was loaded.

I returned to Alabama for revenge, and I found out then that God would fight my battles. I still had temper problems, and I would cut people with a knife if they took advantage of me, hit me, or lied on me. It did not matter, I was mad! Everyone thought I was crazy, but I was crying for help. I just wanted the fear and pain in my heart to go away. Not one person would try to understand what I had been through. They only saw the negative side of me. I was looked at as mean and always wrong about everything that was right. I still did not give up.

Oh, precious moments, how precious it is to fight this winning battle of life that destroys a lot of people. There have been numerous, even by the millions, every day. No one knows the end of this time. Some think they know; some want to know and still don't know and never will know, but I know. I have cried and pleaded too long. Long-suffering is something that is hard to endure, but it is possible through the grace of God. As time went on, I have seen some good and bad, but nothing can compare to the evil wrongdoing that I have seen over the years. Seems like it will never end. As a matter of fact, it will never end until the mighty power says it will end. My heart is so heavy and disappointed. I can't control that. Only one person can do that, and I'm moving on now.

I meet people every day with trouble. I have to go to the pit now, and I am not afraid of it for some reason. Therefore, I know by now that the mighty power is leading me. I am ready to go regardless of what it is. I am ready for the battle. The war is on in 1980 with the missing children in Atlanta, Georgia. Confusing, misunderstood, lack of respect, no morals, no love, no consciousness of being right, no values, no remorse, no understanding, and no place for God. Everything is so unreal and out of control! Children are dying! They have no remorse for human life. You would think that after all of this that something would change.

I began to remember my dreams. Later in life, I realized that my dreams would come to pass. At first I was afraid until April 10, 1998. I began to write things down. A lot happened over the years—signs, visions, and dreams—that I continue to have even today. About two weeks before April 10, I remember calling my mother. I was frightened. My mother was not aware of the fear I had until that day. I had dreams of all kinds of colors of tornadoes. The first tornado was black. The second was gray. The third one was black and white in the middle with a white top and black bottom. The fourth one was white. They were all doming down the river. I was on a boat, and I rose to look. The tornadoes had gone over our heads, and we were safe. I would still see the tornadoes traveling down the fields and river.

I had a delay for two and a half years. I went into work one day at a restaurant. May I add, they fired the black manager because they told her that they had about $3,000 missing. Before this happened, the manager told me that she needed a morning supervisor. I agreed to take the position. I began opening the restaurant every day, filling in for the cook, serving, and helping with dishes. She told me that I would get a raise. Time went by and I had not gotten a raise. I decided to ask the manager again. She replied that the district manager refused to pay me for my duties. I then talked to the district manager myself. I gave him my résumé to apply for the manager position. He decided to hire someone that was not working there even though I was qualified for the job. It was very upsetting, but what can I do? I began to pray to myself for peace. I realized, in thoughts, that I had been denied a job promotion and pay for work that I had done.

My heart is hurting. The pain is intense from crying out to the Lord to help me with this matter. I am realizing I am forty years old and still being discriminated against because of the color of my skin. I feel trapped, and I need to get out. I began to ask the Lord to lead me because I knew he was the only one that could help me. I wanted to fight this battle but with the Lord's help. I did not want to fight this one like I used to fight.

When I was younger, I was called a nigger in Atlanta, Georgia, and also denied pay for my position. I fought with my hands, not understanding that I was wrong also. Now I am back home. After twenty years and not thinking that I would go through something like this again. Flashbacks of past experiences go through my mind. The new manager, Phyllis, came in one day and began to pick at me by making racist remarks, like using the nigger word.

One day, out of the blue, Phyllis said to me, "Brenda, I was just telling George that I am from Niggerville, Ohio."

I replied, "Nogerville?"

She said, "No, Niggerville!"

I couldn't believe what I was hearing. I had a broom in my hand at the time she said it. I held the anger in for the first time. Now I knew not to fight her and that, once again, this was the trick of the devil. I am tired of running. I am going to fight this evil spirit with the power of God. She had the lights fixed so I could not turn them on in the mornings and had the air conditioner on in the middle of winter. I would be so cold. I would not warm up until it was time for me to get off. I realized that she was trying to run me away, but I had faith in God. I knew this time to hold my peace.

I read my Bible and it says, "Vengeance is mine," said the Lord. You know, when you talk about Jesus, the enemy gets mad. I then asked her to show me how to turn on the lights. She said, "We have to 'nigger rig' it." She said it before she knew it, then grabbed her mouth like it was a mistake. My head began to hurt. I knew my blood pressure was going up. This was another test from Satan. I kept my mouth shut and walked away. I was angry but proud of myself for walking off. That didn't run me away. Phyllis began to get mad at me until she finally came out a few days later and asked me to leave. Phyllis Tuder came out and spoke these words to me, "Why don't you just leave because I am not going anywhere!" I told her no, and Satan got madder.

Soon, the KKK came in the restaurant to pick on me. I knew something like this would happen because the district manager, Terry, came in to get my statement. Of course, I reported Phyllis to Terry. Instead of him helping me, he did nothing about it. I knew I was on my own with God's help. Before Terry left the store, he took my picture, and not long after that, the KKK came in the restaurant just about every day to try to run me away. I was afraid for my life. They would come in to curse me and beat the iron plates on the table. They would block the aisles so I couldn't walk by. When I told Phyllis about it, she just smiled and did nothing. I soon had my husband to come to the restaurant until I got off. He came in the restaurant from eight that morning and stayed until two.

I am still praying for strength to get through this matter. Things were out of hand. It would be so cold in the restaurant. Sickness set in my body. My nerves were so bad by now because I had to watch Phyllis keep warm with a space heater while I froze. I had to look at her with that "I don't care" look on her face. By now, I knew what the devil look and act like. I began to think back on what my ancestors had to go through—my mom and other family members, including Henry Wells. His face is in the Carrollton Courthouse window. His face will not go away because he was wrongfully accused of burning the courthouse down. A storm came and ran the mob off.

Carrollton is a small city in Alabama. Henry Wells is my great-great-grandfather's brother whose name is Clifford Wells. I knew Clifford Wells very well as a child. He lived to be, approximately, 126 years old. Everyone lost count. His son was Oscar Wells, who is my mother Laura Hurst's grandfather on her mother's side, Ora Deal Hurst. She married my mother's father, James Hurst. On November 16, 1876, it was said that on Thursday morning, the courthouse was burned. Henry Wells was arrested two years later and died in jail in Carrollton in February 1878. He died from the effects of wounds received while attempting to escape. It was in that same month that the court house windows were put in place. We later learned that Henry Wells was brought back to Carrollton. The citizens of the county were greatly enraged because he was suspected of other and more serious crimes. The crimes were not true. In order to save him from a mob, Henry was hidden in the garret of the courthouse. It was then that a lightning storm came through. Henry was looking out of the window in terror at the angry mob. When the storm had passed, Henry Wells passed on in the garret. No one is sure how he died that day. They remember him saying that he would always be there. His face has been in the

Carrollton Courthouse ever since. They have taken the window out and replaced it with a new one, and his face is still there. In spite of the hailstorm, which destroyed all the other windows, after replacement, the image still remains. It has been scrubbed with soap and rubbed with gasoline by those that don't believe, but it has met every test; the face remains. His face can be clearly seen.

I always knew about the face in the window, but I did not know that he was a family member until 1996. I was told by other family members before they passed on. From my understanding, it was not to be discussed back in the 1800s.

This makes me think on Monday, December 16, 2001. I went in to work. Phyllis sat at the counter every day and just looked at me. The stool at the counter had broken because she would sit there, roll her eyes at me, and talk about me to the customers. On this particular day, I decided to leave a little early because of the stress. When I got home, the tornado siren went off, and the dark clouds rolled in. May I add, I dreamed about tornadoes and saw myself moving some children from the glass door. We left home and went to the shelter. As I sat in this group home, I realized that this was the dream I had. The tornado is on the way. They say it sounds like a train, but they didn't say it sounds like fifty trains! The wind is like a roaring lion. My husband and the elder man that lived in the group home with the resident looked out of the back door and saw it coming. My husband asked me if I wanted to look at it, and I said no. I saw enough in my dream. It is the most powerful thing I had ever seen. I began to pray. My daughter had to get to the floor with my coat covering her head. It was a disaster.

**roadsideamerica.com**

His look of horror still visible....

# Lightning Portrait of Henry Wells

Field review by the editors of

**Carrollton, Alabama**

One of the more bizarre sights anywhere is the face on the courtroom window — aka, the Lightning Portrait of Henry Wells.

Wells, a former slave, was accused of burning the original Pickens County Courthouse in 1876. He was finally arrested two years later. As there was no jail, Wells was placed in the garret of the new courthouse. A mob of locals gathered outside to lynch him.

As Wells peered out the garret window, a bolt of lightning struck nearby and permanently etched his terrified expression into the windowpane. Wells died less than two months later "of wounds received while attempting to escape."

The lightning photo is still visible today, and only from the outside. Up on the third floor, an arrow painted on the outside directs you to the miraculous face.

According to one RA tipster: "Through all the years, in spite of hail and storm, which has destroyed all the windows in the courthouse, this one pane has remained intact. It has been scrubbed with soap and rubbed with gasoline by those who doubt its permanence, but it has met every test and the face remains unchanged. At close

# The Face in the Window and Other Alabama Ghostlore

*Alan Brown*

Both enlightening and entertaining, The Face in the Window is the ?rst scholarly
collection of ghostlore from throughout the state of Alabama. Alan Brown has traveled the
state collecting stories and photographs illustrating the places that gave rise to the eerie
tales. Brown re-creates the experience of actually hearing the tales by reproducing here
each story exactly as it was told. In addition, he includes an analysis of the folk motifs and
themes that run through the ghostlore commonly found in Alabama and examines their
contribution to folk traditions.

*Alan Brown has done an excellent job of collecting ghostlore from throughout Alabama, and as a result, his book
is the most important volume published to date on Alabama ghost traditions.*
-- W. K. McNeil, The Ozark Folk Center

*The Face in the Window is a state-based, genre-focused survey of authentic ghost narratives that will appeal to
readers throughout the South.*
--John A. Burrison, Georgia State University

**Alan Brown** is Associate Professor of English at The University of West Alabama.

176pp., 5 1/2 x 8 1/2, 10 illustrations

ISBN 0-8173-0813-X
paper $19.95t July

---

**How to Order**          **Spring 96 Catalog**          **Home Page**

Tuscaloosa News
March 17, 2008

STAFF PHOTOS | MICHAEL E. PALMER

The historic Pickens County Courthouse has recently been renovated and repainted in the original colors.

# Carrollton residents 'living in another time'

By Marla Luster
Staff Writer

CARROLLTON

Tourists come from as far away as New York City to this Pickens County town to see the face in the window.

But the Pickens County Courthouse window that has the mysterious ghost-like face stamped into it is boarded up, concealed from visitors' curious stares while the historic building is renovated.

That's just fine with Carrollton residents who are convinced that what's most important in their town isn't outlined in a tourist brochure.

"We're living in another time," said Susan Wolfe, county coordinator of the Pickens County Cooperative Library. "Everything gets done without a lot of pressure. It's just a slower-paced environment."

A local pastor likens Carrollton to Mayberry.

"It's the kind of place the police chief may come by and tell you that you left your lights on," said James

The window that holds the famous face at the Pickens County Courthouse has been covered for renovation.

rebuilt in 1877. It was added to the National Register of Historic Places in 1994.

"It looks like it's back in the '60s,"

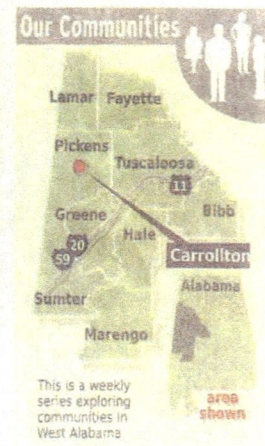

## Our Communities

Lamar  Fayette

Pickens  Tuscaloosa

Greene  Hale  Bibb

Sumter  Carrollton

Alabama

Marengo

This is a weekly series exploring communities in West Alabama

area shown

STAFF GRAPHIC | ANTHONY BRATINA

# CARROLLTON

CONTINUED FROM PAGE 1B

mob. After Wells was arrested for burning down the courthouse two years earlier, a mob gathered to look for him.

A sheriff hid Wells in the newly rebuilt courthouse, but somehow the mob found out he was there.

As Wells stared down at the angry mob, a storm passed over. Lightning struck and scared away the mob. Whether the lightning bolt killed Wells is disputed, but the consensus is that it forever stamped Wells' frightened likeness onto the courthouse window.

Perhaps it's also the town's size that puts people at a slower pace. Carrollton, a perfect square geographically, measures 2 square miles. That places any destination within walking distance, which makes one of the town's newest developments quite useful.

New sidewalks recently replaced grass borders on Alabama Highway 17 North. The development came after senior citizens started walking to get hot 50-cent meals at the Carrollton Nutrition Center on Highway 17.

Senior citizens make up about 25 percent of the population, Mayor John Lammers said. Without a sidewalk, citizens risked their safety walking on a highway where speeds can exceed 55 miles an hour.

"That Highway 17 is a busy highway," Lammers said.

People can also use the sidewalks to walk to the Pickens County Hospital.

Sidewalks already line the storefronts on the main street surrounding the county courthouse in Carrollton's downtown.

In all, Carrollton is home to 35 businesses, including county offices, two small convenience stores, one clothing retailer, one used car dealership/antique store, and a bed-and-breakfast.

Tonya Barringer, the manager of the antique shop, said that antique marbles are a popular item.

STAFF PHOTO | MICHAEL E. P

Carrollton is at the crossroads of Alabama highways 17 and 86. This photo was taken from atop the historic Pickens County Courthouse.

The marbles were made between 1820 and 1837. "In the 1900s they quit making them out of porcelain and started making them out of glass," Barringer said. "New marbles are all made out of glass."

In front of the antique shop/dealership is a row of antique cars. Some were traded in and the family already owned others, Barringer said.

Apparently there isn't much need to slow things down in Carrollton: The town is home to a few stop signs and one stoplight.

"In other words, there's not much to slow you down," said Theodis Henderson, County Extension Agent.

But the lack of stoplights hasn't sped things up in Carrollton, either. Residents do note the lack of entertainment and employment options.

"If we had a Winn Dixie here, we'd have it made," said Annette Williams-Horton, a lifetime Carrollton resident.

Tangie Long, another lifetime resident, said she was disappointed with Carrollton's lack of entertainment outlets. "It's boring," she said. "There's nothing down here for the kids to do."

Long says she travels to Tuscaloosa to go bowling and

shop at Wal-Mart.

Carrollton is approximately 45 minutes west of Tuscaloosa and 30 minutes southeast of Columbus, Miss.

"There are no industries in Carrollton to be competing with," said Tanisia Lavender, Pickens County Hospital's chief operating officer. "Young people leave because there is nothing to do that could afford them a good living."

Lavender's point is backed up by the 2000 Census, which recorded almost a 20 percent drop in the town's population during the past decade.

Beth Goodson, the city clerk, said she doesn't think the population will drop any further, barring any major changes to the town's economic base.

Lavender said the hospital, the town's largest employer, remains critical to the people of Carrollton.

"It's important because it affords healthcare," she said. "Some people go to larger hospitals by choice, but some people can't go to larger hospitals."

Carrollton, along with other cities in Pickens and surrounding counties, is working with the West Central Partnership of Alabama to help attract businesses to the area.

For now, much of the bus takes place in the town's c City Hall is the place to go t the water and gas bills, fines, and traffic tickets.

It also serves as the polic partment, fire department mayor's and city clerk's o Carrollton employs about 13 ple, including four police off the mayor and the city cler

Until a year ago, Goodso helped residents contact p or ambulances in case emergency. Carrollton resi didn't have 911, so they'c Goodson, and she would te police. Now 911 is available

Carrollton also is home new county jail, which will up to 94 prisoners.

Although Carrollton lack nificant industrial develop the town is rich in spiritua lets, as the home of six chu Many of them provide out to the community.

The former pastor of Ca ton Baptist set out years a bring the town's churche gether to better serve the munity.

For years, two predomir white churches, Carrollton tist and Carrollton U Methodist, had worshippe gether for Thanksgiving

After the storm had passed, I heard sirens coming from the direction of my job. I heard on the radio that there was damage in that area. I had my husband drive me there. When I got there, everyone was standing outside. I asked if everyone was all right, and they all replied yes. Thanks to the meat freezer. They got in it for safety. I looked around; the place was torn up. There wasn't anything left standing except the tea I made before I left work. Everyone's car windows were blown out. Eighteen-wheeler trucks were thrown around like toy trucks. A man was sucked out of his truck, and they found him miles away. This storm destroyed 533 homes and 5 businesses. My workplace was one of them. They say the winds were 200 mph! It injured about 75 people and killed 11 people here in Tuscaloosa, Alabama. This made it the single most deadly tornado in the United States that year.

After this happened, it snowed, and Phyllis still wanted us to clean up and get back to work. The ceiling was leaking and still no heat. She still would not close down for repairs. About a month later, the roof caught on fire. The only thing said was we must be on Indian land. Still, she had us working in the freezing cold. Things got so bad until she fired me for no reason. I was then ready to fight back with a lawsuit, which I won in 2003. They closed down a few months after Phyllis fired me (see pictures).

# Tornado was the deadliest in U.S. this year

By EMILIO SAHURIE
emilio.sahurie@tuscaloosanews.com

TUSCALOOSA — In the devastating wake of this weekend's killer tornado, residents continued to dig out from under crushed homes, and officials began the equally mountainous task of assessing the damage.

Saturday's tornado packed winds of nearly 200 mph at times, injured about 75 and killed 11 people here, making it the single most deadly tornado in the U.S. this year.

Included in the death toll were at least two children, and six other children remain at area hospitals.

U.S. Sen. Richard Shelby, a Tuscaloosa County resident, was expected to accompany a team from the Federal Emergency Management Agency today to tour

> *I got my family and that's all that really matters.*
>
> **Angel Turner,**
> whose home was destroyed

the damage. That move could free up millions of dollars in federal grants and loans.

Gov. Don Siegelman, who met with residents Sunday in the Taylorville area, declared a state of emergency in Tuscaloosa County. Accompanied by Sheriff Ted Sexton and emergency personnel, Siegelman talked to FEMA direc-

Please see **TORNADO** Page 8A

# Counseling, comforting await returning students

By CAL MICHAEL
cal.michael@tuscaloosanews.com

TUSCALOOSA — With missing roof shingles as evidence, Englewood Elementary was close to ground zero for Saturday's tornado.

Yet it, as well as the rest of the Tuscaloosa County school system, will be open today, with plans for finishing the 2000 calendar year of classes. The plans for this week also include counseling and comforting students who have suffered terrible losses or are having trouble understanding what has happened to their classmates.

"It is a terrible time for those whom this has happened to, especially because it is around Christ-

mas," said Steve Lamon, Englewood principal.

With only one full day and two half-days left before the holiday break, schools throughout Tuscaloosa County will have counselors on hand for students who are trying to cope with the tragedy unleashed by Saturday's events.

"I am not looking forward to seeing the first names of those who were killed, because I know that I am going to recognize students," Lamon said while looking down at the decimated residential subdivisions that are home for many of his students.

No major structural damage occurred to any of the four schools

Please see **STUDENTS** Page 8A

Dec. 18. 2000    Tuscaloosa News

The Tuscaloosa Water Works tower was one of the few structures that were not damaged when Saturday's tornado struck the [illegible] ...

robert.sutton@tuscaloosanews.c[...]

Tuscaloosa News

Angel Turner's face shows the pain of Saturday's tornado as she looks at one of the few items she was able to salvage from the wreckage of her Bear Creek mobile home — a picture of her husband, Randall, playing T-ball as a child.

## THE STORY BEHIND THE PICTURE

# One image captured heartbreaking toll

■ Photograph of neighbor helping injured girl propels global interest.

**By KATHERINE LEE**
katherine.lee@tuscaloosanews.com

TUSCALOOSA — It was a simple act of charity that propelled Mike Harris onto the front pages of newspapers and Web sites around the world.

A day after a tornado killed at least 11 people in south Tuscaloosa, the Tuscaloosa News photo of Harris carrying a young girl away from the ruin of what was once her home became a symbol of the wide path of destruction the tornado tore through the city.

Media outlets around the world searched Sunday for Harris and the girl he rescued, identified as 6-year-old Whitney Crowder. Whitney and her 3-year-old sister, Abby, remained in critical condition in a pediatric intensive care unit at Children's

Please see **IMAGE** Page **8A**

Mike Harris of Tuscaloosa carries Whitney Crowder, 6, from the rubble of the Bear Creek Road Trailer Park Saturday. Both were unidentified when this photograph ran on the front page of Sunday's Tuscaloosa News.

Tuscaloosa News

ECCENTRIC AMERICA
Roadside oddities

Search this site:

SEARCH

**The Random Oddity**

Lonestar Brewery

Home
**About Mark**
Somalia
**Submit a Picture**
**Roadside Links**
**Site Search**

**Bookmark This Site**
( IE users only )

**Alabama**
Carrollton
Dothan
Troy

**Arizona**
**California**
**Colorado**

• Back

**The Lightning Portrait of Henry Wells**
**Carrollton, Alabama**

Click on any of the images below to view a larger size.

(Reprinted from the historical marker outside the Courthouse)

...A freedman, Henry Wells, was accused of burning the second (courthouse) on November 16, 1876. He was arrested in January, 1878, and held in the garret of this building. Legend holds that as Wells peered out of the North window at a mob gathering below, lightning struck nearby, indelibly etching his image on the pane.

I've seen the story a few times, and I have to say that it never seems to change. This thing was pretty damned eerie to look at. Although the courthouse was closed when I arrived into town, there is a telescope nearby that, for .25 cents, you can peer up and see the window image quite clearly.

# The Face in The Window
### or
# The Ghost in the Garret

On November 16th, 1876, Thursday morning, the courthouse was burned. Henry Wells was arrested two years later and died in jail in Carrollton, in February, 1878, from the effects of wounds received while attempting to escape. It was in that same month that the Court House windows were put in place. But, you ask, what has that to do with the face in the window?

It is a queer thing that repetition without contradiction often comes to be taken as truth, and in this case a story has been so often repeated that it is here set down, at least as partly true. So draw near and we will tell it to you as it was told to us.

It is said that when Henry Wells was brought back to Carrollton the citizens of the county were greatly enraged, for he was suspected of other and more serious crimes that that of burning a Court House. To save him from the outraged mob Henry was hidden in the garret of the new Court House. It was then that an electric storm passed over-just when Henry was looking down in terror upon those gathered in the square below-and Henry's face was stamped as indelibly upon that pane as through a photographer had opened his lens and likeness. Whether it is a good likeness of Henry or not may be a matter of some dispute, but it certainly pictures all the emotions the unfortunates negro must have experienced- horror, sorrow and pain.

And some people say that on stormy nights when the wind makes weird noises around the eaves of the Court House, one can see by the glare of the lighting the ghost of Henry Wells peering out of the garret window on the North side of the Court House.

Through all the years, in spite of hail and storm which destroyed all the other windows, this particular pane with its striking image remains. It has been scrubbed with soap and rubbed with gasoline by those who doubt its permanence, but it has met every test and the face remains unchanged. At close range it is as other panes in the sash, clear and flawless. It has been viewed from the ground-viewed from the spot where once gathered an angry mob--that the face can be clearly seen.

**Seeing is believing.**

I can understand things much better now. I can also understand the works that God has for me to do. Like understanding how my sister beat her crack cocaine addiction. I came back to Alabama for a while and returned to Atlanta to find my sister fighting for her life. I went to the home where she and her two boys were living. I found out that the young lady who owns the house was also smoking crack with my sister. I got sick to the stomach to see my sister in this predicament. I began to pray, asking God to please make a way so I can help my sister and her two boys get out of this home.

I soon got a job at the nursing home. After I got on, I took my sister to apply for a job. We both were working. We were both able to get a place of our own. Yet the devil would not leave my sister alone. We had to go to war with this one. I can say that through it all, my sister is doing fine today. In 2003, Satan was mad because of the blessings that God has for her in 2004. She called me one day, thinking that she had pulled a muscle in her side. It got worse and fever set in. I went to see her. She was coughing hard, and I began to think that she had pneumonia. Her doctor, Dr. Ebony Pratt, diagnosed her with a pulled muscle instead of doing an X-ray to be sure. Dr. Pratt showed no interest in giving her one. I got very concerned because I knew that it was something else. By the way, my sister and I are like twins. We dressed like twins when we were small children. If my mother bought one, the other one would get the same. Now I am really concerned, so I called the doctor myself. They finally took an X-ray and found fluid in her lungs. Because of the fever and cough, Dr. Pratt sent her back home and gave her some medicine.

By the way, she had already been sick with this for two weeks now. Three weeks has gone by and the fever and cough are worse. Dr. Pratt still ignored my sister's health. It's praying time. The enemy was still at her. She went to the emergency room, and Dr. Pratt did not show up. I had to practically make them admit her in the hospital. After they admitted her, they did X-rays. They found that she had double pneumonia. Antibiotics were not helping. I demanded another doctor. Dr. Pratt wanted to put a feeding tube in her neck, but I said no. By now, no food is staying down. I had her put on Ensure, a heath drink. Dr. Pratt got upset and said she was only going to throw it up. After we had a specialist come in, they found out that the medications were not working. My sister had two pus pockets in her right lung; therefore, the doctors had to do surgery and put a tube in her lungs and into the pus pockets to pump them out.

I was really praying, giving it my all. My mom and my big brother, Pastor Billy Wayne Hurst, were also praying. I was very proud and looked up to him a lot. The doctors removed one pus pocket but weren't sure if they could remove the other one. Prayer was the key once again. My sister gained a lot of weight back.

Still going to church and still standing on the Word of God, I was losing weight from all the stress from my lawsuit.

My mother beat breast cancer. I lowered my cholesterol, and I was off my cholesterol medicine. No more medicine for stress or acid reflux. The waters were slowing down, the winds were picking up, my steps were getting longer, and my days were growing near. Peace was coming to me. My health was poor, but I was still standing strong. My family was coming together in the spirit of God and still holding on to God's Word, which we believe in truly.

So many are leaving this world between 2000 and 2003. Now it is 2004, and may God bless my soul. I have finally been blessed. My soul says, "Yes, Lord!" The wrong doings that Phyllis did to me finally paid off. I was awarded enough money to buy the home that I dreamed about. It sits up on a hill with brick and vinyl siding. It has a two-car drive, car port, five bedrooms, three bathrooms, kitchen, living room, washroom, an in-ground pool, two patios, large backyard, circle drive around the back, greenhouse, a workshop for my husband, and two storage rooms. God has made a way once again! My key point is never give up on the Lord no matter what anyone does to you or say about you. Just have faith and believe. My family does!

# CAME TO ATLANTA, WOKE UP, NOW 'M WRITING

The elevations are rising. Storms are still coming. I am in Atlanta, Georgia, at this time to get a break from it all. Maybe now I can analyze everything, exhale, and go on. I am still standing in the gap for my family. This is July 8, 2005.

I am watching the news. They talked about the storm that is on the way called Hurricane Dennis. People are coming to Atlanta Georgia from Florida and Mobile Alabama because the storm is coming. It is coming off the coast of Florida and Jamaica. Will they survive this storm like the last storm? Only God knows. So I pray for everyone to be safe through these crying times. Rising waters are here. People are afraid, but I do believe that everyone cried out to the Lord and was told that everything will be all right.

My business is coming along okay. I will not stop for that great day and make sure I do not walk away from what the Lord told me that some will learn the way, some may not wake up the next day. Can people hear what I say as I am going the last miles of the way? So I'll just pray that everyone will hear someday.

I had the first-year anniversary of my restaurant business. As of June 22, 2005, things are looking better, people are trying to hold me back because of jealousy. They are looking at the outside and not on the inside. Some people think I owe them something. I will survive this trial because I like to win.

Atlanta has a flash flood warning. At this time, the lighting is still flashing and the thunder is still rolling. Are we listening? Who is listening? By the way, my brother was told that he had clogged arteries in his head around the temple area. Doctors did a biopsy and set a date for surgery. Now when he went for the surgery, they could not find the clogged arteries. God is still good and always and always will be. My mother is becoming very strong. Her nerves have gotten bad from the chemotherapy that she had for cancer. Now she is smiling again. "Never give up, never give up" is in my heart and soul. Let's teach this at this time. I am still in Atlanta. I am down the street from Comfort Inn, peeping up the street at Days Inn. I used to work there, and I am thinking back on the day they fired me for wearing braids, and I refused to take my hair down. Discrimination.

# Brenda's

# Home Town Deli

Again I am across the street from the waffle house. Back in the '80s, my step nephew had gotten a job there where I worked also. He was a dishwasher on this hot sunny day. The evening supervisor came through the door. My step nephew was on the phone, trying to get a ride home. The supervisor walked up to him and said, "Get off of that blank phone, boy." I felt and seen the hurt on this young child. I then told the supervisor that he was wrong in a firm way, and he fired me. That was okay because he needed to be told the truth. You do not disrespect children or anyone just because they do not have the same color skin. The tone in his voice and the look on his face showed so much anger. I forgive, but I guess I will never forget because I have a mind too just like others. I think too! I am a human being just like the rest. Our bodies get sick. We get weak, we lack, and we crack just like others. In other words, some things I can't tell and won't to tell but can't tell. Nobody knows the trouble I have seen.

I used to run track for Riverside Junior High School in Tuscaloosa, Northport, Alabama, the home of the Crimson Tides. May I add Roll Tide also? I ran track at Stillman College during upward-bound summer program. Let me explain, while in Atlanta, Georgia, I was twenty years old at the time, singing in a group called Sassy, traveling from Atlanta to Tennessee. From there to Tuscaloosa, then back to Atlanta, having fun and seeing dreams come true, meeting the famous. I was working at a coffee shop at American Hotel in downtown Atlanta. In the coffee shop, sitting at one of my tables are the globe-trotters. A lot is going through my mind at this time. I enjoy serving them, and they made me feel very comfortable. Before they left, they gave me a picture with their autograph on it. Also had an autographed picture of Red Fox. He was at the Atlanta Hilton Hotel.

I also had a run-in with Greg Brady in the elevator. Other young ladies were going down to the first floor also.

One of the young ladies asked her friend, "Is that Greg Brady?" And as soon as she said yes, everyone started to run behind him. I did not follow. It is not my style to get overly excited, but I do feel very happy that I had the chance to see him for a short time. I had also worked at the Atlanta Omni and had seen the Atlanta Hawks, basketball games, and concerts with special guest like Bruce Springsteen and had the greatest encounter and the privilege to see Michael Jackson himself and realized that he was bad. With the silver gloves on, I was standing in the doorway with my binoculars, not missing one move of his feet, and believe me, he was bad. As I got off work, walking underground going to the Marta train station, people are everywhere. Some were crying and passing out. It was something like a dream.

Out of the blue, here comes Michael riding in a black Explorer or something to that nature. People really got emotional as he drove past them. As he passed me, I waved and smiled, and he waved back at me and smiled and that was enough for me, but as I walked on, policemen were escorting Michael through the crowd. As they got to the corner to turn, a lady ran in front of one of the horses that the police was riding, and the horse fell on top of her. It was hilarious. As I walked further, a cameraman asked me and others to stand and just yell and wave our hands. That was easy. He said that it would be in one of Michael's videos. I never knew which one. It did not matter. I was pleased to have had the privilege to get that close to him, being the big star that he is. Then I move in life in Atlanta and decided to become a medical assistant. I love it. I graduated in 1985 from Draughons College on Peachtree Street. My mother came from Tuscaloosa. She was very proud. My sister went to the same school, and we finished at the same time.

# VISITING ATLANTA AND THINKING BACK

Before all of this occurred, a boyfriend in Atlanta did not know about my running abilities. He came to the apartment where I lived, off Cascade Road. As he approached me, I noticed the expressions changing on his face. My sister and I was talking to my mother long-distance on a pay phone. And as he got closer to me, he reached out and hit me on my face with his fist. I had to tell my mother to hold on so I could deal with this matter. I struck out on him and told him to never come near me again. May I remind you my sister was there also. So you can about imagine what we did to handle that.

Days went by, I thought that he had learned his lesson. Instead, he showed up at my home as I returned from the grocery store. He pushed me through the door as I attempted to open it and began to hit me in my head. Food was all over the floor. I knew I had to really come on with it. In my mind, I said Jesus, and after that, I remember I had turned on my dishwasher before I left to go to the grocery store. He had pushed me back on the love seat that sit as you come into the door. I pushed myself up against the wall and pushed him to the floor, kicking him away from me. I then ran into my kitchen and went straight to the dishwasher, and as I raised up and turned around, his eyes were as big as half a dollar, and he ran and ran all the way down Cascade Road, and every time he stops and look back, I was right behind him. I'm thinking the track paid off because I refused to live in a city away from home and be afraid of getting attacked by a boy just because he thought that I was talking to another boy on the phone.

And all the time that I was running behind him, I'm thinking my mother is in Tuscaloosa, Alabama, worried about me because of him. That made me not want to stop running, and I am saying he will never do this again. He was so tired by the time I ran about a mile and one block away from the street that he lived on. His sister called me the next day and told me that he was in the hospital because he caught pneumonia from sweating and running so long, but he knew not to stop. Thank God that he didn't. And on top of it all, I was good and tired of being abused. Running track gave me power in my legs, and I thank God for giving me the strength to keep running. I never had problems out of him anymore. I haven't thought about this in years. Visiting here is bringing some memories to my mind. I have been here in Atlanta visiting for two days now, and I can hear it and see it. Once again, it is coming. Are we praying? It is so amazing that, somehow, this strong power of love is overflowing through my heart, letting me know that I am loved. When you can't see it but you can feel it, that is love, and that's what keep me going. I know I am loved.

My soul weeps as the August 2005 Hurricane Katrina comes through. The storms are still coming. Are we listening, looking, or thinking? The next day, while in Atlanta, I was looking at the news in my hotel room and had seen where the storm had destroyed— New Orleans. Floodwater everywhere, people are hungry, needing food, water, clothes, and shelter. It is so sad. What is God trying to show us? I dreamed of the earth spinning toward the east fast as it could move. I guess this is sign of all the hurricanes that I have seen lately.

On June 14, 2005, I dreamed that I was on my back patio grilling with a cousin, and the further I went toward the backyard, I looked out and saw red, like fire, in the middle of the clouds and a voice came out from it and said, "I am Lord. I have given people jobs and they have quit, but it will not be acceptable." Now I am asking myself, was he saying that he was tired of people not doing what he ask of them? We all have a purpose here on earth. He has different jobs for all of us. My job from God is to foster care in my home, help people, give encouraging words, and tell people of his goodness. And I know that God will not harm us. Maybe it started with Adam and Eve. And I also know that Jesus died for our transgressions.

I never experienced a dream to this effect before. I can't believe I heard a voice from heaven. It was so real. As the Lord was speaking, the wind was blowing rain everywhere as well as thunder and lightning, and I did not get wet and my grill was still burning. I looked down at the grill, and I could see a ball of fire. I see little plus signs on my paper that looked like little crosses to me, but I did not type that so I will leave it there. This is a wonderful experience.

I have been doing foster care for eight years now, and I know if it was not because of the Lord, I could not do this with all the different behaviors and watch them come and go after you have bonded with them, but that's my job from the Lord. Seeing them hurting. My daughter, Chassade Shambriea, also helps other children, and she is just a child herself. I see it every day how she cares and help the children be happy. She is eleven years old now, and I always pray that she makes the right decisions. And I give her pep talks and encouraging words every day and try to show her the right way to go. She is an honor student and won the excellence award. There isn't enough room on the wall for all of them. She achieved them over the years. I always make room for my baby, precious she is to me. But now, I do know my mom did the same thing with me and I grew up and made some mistakes, and by her being human, I know she will make mistakes too.

I wasn't supposed to have babies, but I have Chassade, my pride and joy. I know that I should not love anything or anybody before God, but I am still glad to say that I have a child that I can love so dearly. Some people may say that I am overprotective of her, but I call it love. I know what's out there, and it is also my job to teach her as though the Lord has been teaching me. Some people say that I am crazy. I'm I crazy for obeying my Father above? I am getting older. I will be forty-six next month, October 23, and I am, at the time in my life, where I am getting comfortable with my encounters. I am more relaxed. I have had a hard battle trying to have my babies. I was pregnant with my son, Joquel Terra! After losing him, it was a hard fight, being in labor for two days and a half. And knowing that my baby is not alive inside of my stomach, it broke me completely down, but the prayers and myself talking to the Lord about it brought me through. I had a visit from my son every year around his birthday. He does certain things to let me know that he is with me and that gives me a sense of peace. He lets me know that he is okay.

If I told everyone what he does or what happens around his birthday, they would have a hard time believing it, and I have some witnesses too. My daughter has told me about some things he has done to let her know that he is okay also. I have learned over the years that the battle is not mine; it's the Lord's. I listen to the song all the time. I have found peace within myself, peace that I had to find for myself. Now I know I can't find peace in others, only in the Lord, and I can conquer. Now I know how to rest in the Lord, and as far as my dreams, I did not ask for them. They were given to me, and I know that they do not come from humans. We learn when we listen.

I am thinking about Noah when the Lord told him to build the ark. It was rough on him, but he builds it. This is February 2006. I was working at my deli, which is inside of Home Town Grocery, doing it all myself. Can't get good help. People are stealing from me no matter how much I help them, so I learn to do it myself. One day, an officer came to the deli, and his name badge said Wells. I began to ask him about his last name, and he told me his family was from Gordo, and his grandparents were Wells, and they were the same Wells that went to church with my grandparents, and my mother went to school with her, played, and stayed overnight with his aunt down in Gordo when they were children. Should I say I just put some pieces together? I know this is for a reason.

On February 5, 2006, I woke up that morning remembering the dream I had the night before. I dreamed that I looked up to the sky and I saw candy that was big and round spinning like a spinning top. It looked like peppermint candy in a big circle, very thick on a white cloud. It was red and white. It seemed as though everyone was running, trying to find shelter, and some people had problems finding a place to go because they were swinging so fast, and it seemed that they would soon swing a loose from the candy that look like rope. I made it to my house, and people followed me. It seemed like we couldn't go through the doors. We had to go through the window that was on the left side of the house. My sister found a window that was open. I saw some smaller windows and wondered why were they so small, so we all went through the window that my sister *found*. After we went inside, I had a room for everybody, and I plan for the children to sleep two at the head of the bed and two at the foot of the bed. It seemed as though other people came, and they were coming up on my front porch, and they were out in the yard. I asked them to come in because I had room for more, but not all of them. The skies got quiet, so I looked outside and then up to the sky, and I saw faces as though it could be Jesus. There were three faces, and below that, I saw Satan. He didn't know that I was aware of his presence. Jesus's head was lying to the right as though he was asleep on all three faces, and I knew that he knew that I had seen him.

Other people and I went back inside, and the candy spun a loss with a mighty wind, and it got quiet again, and I looked out the window and the candy, looking like rope, formed into my backyard like big and long bridge, shining as high as the sky and as pretty red-and-white peppermint candy that led up to my back door.

It was like rope threaded down the sides like the form of a bridge that you would see in the jungle. People were coming from all around north, south, east, and west. There were so many, and I was trying to figure out how I was going to find sleeping room for all these people. I thought I did not have enough room for everyone, but when I got them inside, I had plenty of room. I wonder, what is God trying to show me? Only time will tell.

Now I am thinking about all the people that I have cared for over the years, and I will always make room for the needy. I care for them and teach them about God's way, not my way, because I am human and could never be perfect, except in my heart. I have a lot on me every day, growing tired, but somehow, God always make a way for me to keep doing my purpose here on earth. My mother, Laura, always tells me that God got more for me to do, and it's true. I've already had over fifteen foster children plus my daughter, family, and friends that I'm always helping, and the great thing about it is I love helping people. Now my mission is to help my daughter. She is in a group called Dancing Stars, which allows her to be in the Stillman College parade and the Christmas parade every year and to perform at different theaters. And now we are working on the disruptions, and I can say I love my child and will always be there for her as my mother did for me, and she is still there for me. She is thirteen now, and I ask God to please put his angels all around her and to lead her in her everyday life.

Before I *moved back home* to Tuscaloosa, I lived in Indiana. I never knew my grandmother on my dad VL's side, but I had an aunt that they called Aunt Cat. She was like a mother to my dad and his siblings. That's all we knew about Aunt Cat at that time, and later, I got to know my grandmother Rosetta's sisters, Aunt Helen and Aunt Dolly. Aunt Cat was always smiling, laughing. She loved to feed you with a smile. She had twelve children plus a lot of grand- and great-grand and some great-great-grandchildren and us, and she loved each and every one of us and treated us with respect and love. If you needed her, she was always there. She even kept my baby sometime when I had to work.

My grandmother Rosetta only have one sister still living, and that is Aunt Helen down in Gordo, Alabama. And I can say I see where my siblings and I got the dancing from. We love music, like all my aunts and uncles on my dad's side of the family. Every last one of them can dance or were dancers sometime on another in their life, starting from Mississippi up to Birmingham, ALABAMA. My sister and I danced on all the talent shows. We would win first place all the time. We were living in Northport, Alabama, where we were raised. We would participate in all the talent shows. After we win, the ones here in Tuscaloosa would always start a fight with us, but that did not stop us. They took us to Fayette College to perform. It was fun, but that still did not stop us from singing in the New Zion Baptist Junior Choir back in the 1970s and 1980s. We were also on a TV show that came on every Wednesday like the *Soul Train Show*, but they called it the *Ebony Express*. We would always show up with our stacked shoes on and wearing Afros and braids. It was here in Tuscaloosa that my aunt Helen was still dancing, and Aunt Dolly did too.

Back to Aunt Cat, it did not matter if she had Auntie Dot's children or Auntie Beaulah's children. She welcomes us all. That made me feel loved by her, and I knew that she loved my child. She was married to one of my grandmother's brother, Foster Sr. She passed on in 2006. I'll always have the memory of being in her home eating, drinking coffee early in the morning, and with all the children, grandchildren, nieces, and nephews, on top of that, the family friends. If you want to see family, it was the place to go. Now when it comes to her kids, some of them have up to fifteen or more children. Some had ten children and twins more the one set. I will always love my family. When my grandmother Rosetta died, my dad and his siblings were just children. The youngest two do not remember their mother at all.

My uncle Sonny Boy, they called him, told me the story, and he said that my grandfather Guss Lee had bought a new horse buggy and wagon. They all were standing on the front porch. He put my grandmother Rosetta on the wagon and attempted to take her for a ride. All the children were standing on the front porch looking, and when the children began to clap their little hands because they were excited, that spooked the horse and my grandmother fell off the back of the wagon. As she hit the ground, the older children and my grandfather went to help her up off the ground, and a stick was stuck in her head. She died, so I never knew her and had not even seen a picture of her. Aunt Dolly told me that the only picture they had was burned up in a house fire years ago. So that left my dad and his siblings to be separated and went to different family members like aunts, and later, they all came back together as they got older, and some of the younger ones went to live with the older siblings. That's why I try not to judge people because no one knows what other people go through. One thing I can say is, my auntie Dot, the youngest of the siblings, will call me long-distance and find me when she comes to the south and visit, and that reminds me that she is concerned and cares about me. My aunt Pearl does too, the one everybody in the family says that I look like when she was younger. She is sixty-seven now, and she can still dance and take it to the floor.

Music and dancing and singing keep us relaxed. I am glad to know my family on my daddy's side. That filled a great void in my life to see people that favored me and like to do some of things that I like to do, filling in a missing piece in my life. And by the way, we called my father VL, my daddy. My father's brother moved back home from Indiana. He was ill from Alzheimer's disease. He cannot think like he used to. I used to have patients with that disease, and I know a lot about it. He begin to fall all the time, so I moved him in with me after he left the nursing home, and I'm looking at my father's brother living in my home, saying to myself, what a blessing to have this time with my uncle.

A few months went by, he was walking again, and we would dance if a song came on the radio. He would always say, "Come on, sugar. Let's dance." And we would cut a rug as the old saying goes. And we would dance sometimes until the whole *song* went off. He can *dance*. His sister, my aunt Pearl, came down from Detroit to visit him, and he danced with her, and they can really do the old dances together. My uncle's feet could move fast as lightning. You cannot keep up with those dance moves that they do. I enjoyed watching them dance. It would remind me of myself. Now Uncle Sonny Boy's legs were getting stronger. He began to walk without the walker. I wanted my dad to live with me before he passed on, but he was too sick to leave the nursing home. He was having at least eight seizures a day, and he had Alzheimer's.

Some people are talking negative, thinking about money and lying. But I don't care because I do things to help my people because I love my people, and I do things from my heart with true love and honesty. I do not think that my uncle really understands his condition. I just try to make him feel welcomed and that my home is his home. He is at peace now. I had a godmother who was only five years older than I was. She lived across the street from me when I was seven years old, and she was thirteen. She was fun, always happy, and very strong willed. Her name was Brenda Sue, the same as mine. I remember when she used to keep my sister Edna and my younger brother Robert and I. My older brother, Billy, was old enough to see about himself. When my mother would go to work, she would cook and clean for us, and she would look out for us.

We were in the projects at this time because the county tore down the houses where we used to live in to build a new school called Matthew Elementary, and when we were living there, the old Matthew was across the street from where we lived, so we were given two storage apartments to rent. We lived there until my mother found another house. We had to fight all the time. The children were picking at us all the time, but I earned my respect, if you know what I mean. My mother loved Bren. That's what we called her. She did a good job as our sitter, and sometimes, she would take us across the street to her house after her mother had cooked, and she would set the table for her seven children that she had still living at home at that time. It did not matter. She would always invite us to eat too. Later, we would go over to the old Matthews school to pick pecans and play on the merry-go-round. She also taught my sister Edna and I how to put our dance steps together and make a routine, and that helped us later in life to participate in talents shows as we grew up.

After we grew up, we moved away and later moved back home. We would always find Bren and get together to eat, dance, talk about the old days, and have the best time. Later, she became ill and passed on at the age of fifty-three in 2007. She would always come to my restaurant to patronize. She had become ill, and the doctors could not do anything else for her. She died the same day that my aunt Cat died, and their funeral was on the same day. It was hard, but I got through it. At Bren's funeral, they had big lights hanging from the ceiling, and one of them started to sway from side to side. I asked my husband if he saw that, and he said yes. I knew then that Bren was all right.

I thank God for giving me the opportunity to have someone like Bren in my life. I miss her so much, but I think of all the times that she told me the good Lord knows through it all, and before she left, she was still cooking food and invited us over for a feast and, once again, dancing and singing. And now we are praising the Lord too. And I always love to hear her say as we walked through the door, "Are y'all hungry?" It just made me feel right at home, like in my younger days and always had fun. It was like going back around people that really know you and cared about you and gave good advice about life's problems and encouraged us to be good girls. She would say even though we were grown ladies now, we were still her girls. That takes me back to thinking of the positive role models in my life, such as my aunt Nettie. We all call her. She was my grandfather's sister and was always at the prayer meeting that my grandmother Ora Deal Hurst, my mother's mother, had every Tuesday in her home, and later, after she died, my grandfather began to have the prayer meeting every Christmas Eve and that kept the family together so we would see Aunt Nettie at every meeting.

She would take my sister, my stepsisters, and I for a ride in her car. She loved to drive, and back then, she would keep her a pint of whisky under her car seat, and she would reach under her seat to take a little nip, not letting us see it because we always sit in the backseat, but we knew, and once she get her nip, she would take off in the car, spinning rubber, and zoom we went. My stepsister liked it. She would say hit it Aunt Nettie, and she would take off across the Black Warrior Bridge. We were not afraid because she was known around town for being one of the best drivers around these parts. That was her way of spending time with us and letting us know that she loved us. And we always went to her house to see her and Uncle Will with my mother and father. Everyone enjoyed her because she was fun and always kept us laughing by saying funny things.

She passed away in October 2006. When we attended her funeral, the pastor spoke on her, saying Mrs. Netty was a faithful member and always paid her tithes on Sunday, and when she was sick, she would send her tithes to church. But when she did attend church and when service was over, you had better get out of the way. Everyone would say, "Here comes Ms. Netty." I sit by my uncle Oscar, my mother's oldest brother. I could see him turning his head, looking at me from time to time.

He was so dear, the sweetest thing you could meet. He knew a lot about the Bible and the Lord, just downright godly. He attended all the prayer meetings on Christmas 2006. He stood up to tell his testimony and told us again about Henry Wells, smiling and not showing any signs of feeling bad, but he was so happy and told us that flowers were growing in his backyard and he had his son take a picture of them. I knew that it was a sign from God but did not know what this meant, and he told me he always prayed and asked the Lord for my protection. That was the last prayer meeting that he attended. He died from diabetes on January 5, 2007, which was only two weeks after the last prayer meeting he attended. Through it all, he would come to my restaurant after his dialysis on Fridays to get his chitterlings, and that made me feel good. And I was thinking back when he took me to the hospital when I went through Riverside High School's front glass. He was there then and still there for me in his own way, not counting the sweet potato pies that he would give me when I came home to visit and stop by to see him when I lived in Atlanta, Georgia.

In this last prayer meeting with my uncle Oscar, he stood up without his cane as though he did not have a pain in his body. He really talked about Henry Wells to us a lot, and I thank him for that. Now I know that he was telling me this for a reason and giving me the history of my family. He told us everything that he knew, and I asked him why did this take so long to come out, and he stressed to me that back in those days, they were always told to keep it hush-hush. Now I understand.

I know that I was told because I am the one that is chosen to tell this great secret with no shame. I ask myself, why me? Where is Henry Wells buried? Will this heal the family of shame, hurt, and scars from not being able to talk about this great man all these years? Will this heal Henry Wells? Will the truth be told? I used to feel a little fear, but after I went through a situation myself, which built my faith, the fear went away. I think my family has been tormented enough. We love everyone and God, and that is no reason to be afraid of the truth.

I was married to a man from Africa. He was a good husband, but there is one thing that I do not like, and that is when his best friend tried to hit on me. I told my husband at the time about it, and he took up for his friend, and that did it. I could not stay with him after that, so we had a bad fight, and I asked him to leave.

After five years together, I moved back to Tuscaloosa, got my divorce, and moved back to Atlanta. I went to wok at the Omni. One afternoon, I was making pretzel. I looked up and saw morning doves all over the roof in the area that I was working, and the roof was made of glass. You can see the clouds. It was beautiful.

The next evening, I was on my way to work. As the train passed in between stations, I looked out of the window and saw Jesus standing on the side of the bridge. His hair was jet-black. He had on a long black robe and black sandals with straps around his leg. He was looking down. I could not see his face, but I could see the color of his skin, and it was the color of brass glowing like gold. I then noticed the man sitting in front of me. He had salt-and-pepper hair. I leaned forward, and I asked him if he saw that. He said yes. When the train stopped at the Omni station, I looked all around to talk to the man about what we had seen, and he was nowhere to be found. I went to work that evening wondering.

The next day, on my way, I looked over to see if I would see him again. I did not, but I could not understand how he stood up in that small spot. I knew then that Jesus is everywhere, not just in one place but everywhere. That was a relief to my mind, but at the time, I did not know that I was getting ready to go through something I never thought would happen to me-another big test. Will I pass this one?

The next day, I woke up with a bad toothache. It was so bad that I could not go into work that day. The next day, it was so bad that the infection had gotten into my sinus and had the left side of my face swollen so big. My eye was closed shut, and I was running like I had a bad cold. I was in so much pain by now that I had to go to the hospital. After the doctor had seen me, he told me that he would have to do surgery later. After the infection cleared up, I went home in pain, worse than ever. It got so bad my mother Laura my aunt Eunice had to come. I knew then, regardless how things look, that everything was going to be all right. My mother, being faithful to God and serving Jesus like she does, when she enters a room, you can feel the presence of the Lord. The day of the surgery, my mom went with me. I cried all the way there, and all the way back home, my mother sat on the sofa. I put my head on her lap. By now, I was taking pain pills like candy. My mom said to me, "You are taking too many." I just needed the pain to go away. I was in pain for three weeks. My mom finally gave me what I needed— prayer. After that, I was prepared to go to Indiana to take care of my father. He was very ill. This is 1989. I then got a job at the nursing home that he was in. I did not like the way the workers would treat him. I would defend him, and they reported me as though I was doing something to them, and I could not understand how the staff would allow things like this to go on. They finally fired me, but that was okay. I could not stand by and watch people pick at my father.

Later, while in Indiana, I became a member of a church called Harvester Word of Life, and there my life changed. He would always tell his members that it does not matter if things looked like they have gone crazy and to still put your trust in God. And he would also tell us that greater is he that is in you than he that is in the world, and he said I am going to keep on telling you, and he would repeat it over and over. This time in my life, I wanted to have a baby. I was about twenty-nine and married again because my family does not believe in shacking up, they call it. One Sunday, we had a guest speaker and my pastor his wife and the guest speaker begin to ask people that needed prayer about something to come down front my sister looked back at me.

I felt she knew that I was going down for prayer when I stood up. My sister looked as though she knew that this was it. I had the faith because Pastor William would always tell us to stop saying what is not going to happen and start speaking what we want to happen. I started telling people on my job that I was going to have a baby. They would look at me very funny, but I had my faith in God. In fact, I became fertile three months after they prayed for me. I was afraid for some reason. I guess I could not believe it either. I knew and everyone that knew I could not have a child has seen evidence of what the Lord our God can do. I would hold my stomach all the time even when I was in the choir stand singing. Everything went well in the beginning until my ninth month.

Two weeks before I was due, I asked the doctor to let me have my baby now, and he did not. He thought that I was anxious being that this was my first, but that was not it. I felt that he needed to come out right then, but no one believed me, and sure enough, my baby died. I could not understand why go this long and let me down. Aaaaaaaaaaaaaaaaaa! I had his funeral, and all my family and the few friends that I had came to support me. I knew not to question God. I knew it was for a reason, but being a human being, I did have problems dealing with my loss. My nerves were bad by now. Even if my hair touched my skin, I would jump. My aunt who lived in Saint Louis, Massachusetts, sent me a bell as a gift. It had the Lord's Prayer on it. As my husband and I sat in the living room trying to understand what was going on, the bell came off the tall stand and landed right in front of us, ringing as it landed. Sitting straight up, my husband looked at me and I looked at him, and we both said, at the same time, "Joquel," which was our son's name. I knew he was there and would always be around, but I still needed answers.

The encounter with my son continued like now as I am writing this. That eighteen A's that you see in this book, I did not do that. As I am tying, I so happen to look up, and it was there. I know it is my son letting me know he is still okay and will always be okay. I then became angry and underwent all the stages that a person go through when they are grieving. After all the pain, I still needed answers. Anything, at this point, will do, so I begin to talk to my spiritual counselor, and she told me that my son was in the wrong place, and the doctors told me that there was no just cause. He just stopped breathing. I felt somehow good enough to go back to church and work. At this time, I was working at the Fort Wayne State Developmental School as I passed medication to my clients. I could feel tears about to roll down my face as they line up, walk up to the cart, and say "Hey, Brenda" with a big smile on their faces, looking at me as though they were glad to see me.

I did not realize how much I miss them too. I loved them all. Some were mildly mentally retarded and some were severe. Every day now, I am praying, "Lord, if you give me a child that died, I know you can give me one that will live." And it came to my mind, what are you going to give me? I want something from God, so I got to give him something and not put anything before God, not even my child. Now I am beginning to understand what I have read in the Bible. You do not, by all means, put anything before him. He is all our Father, so I asked, "Lord, what would you have me do?" And it came to my mind that I got to make a vow with the Lord.

I then asked God, "What would you have me do?"

"You sing. Yes, tell the people of my goodness and make a joyful noise unto the Lord."

An instrument came to my mind, and I am saying to myself, I do not know how to play an instrument.

One day, my husband asked me if I wanted to ride with him to the music store. I want to get out of the house to try and get past the depression I was going through. As I walked through the door, I saw a tambourine hanging on the wall. I asked the store clerk to let me see it, and I bought it.

When I got home, I said, "Lord, I do not know how to play a tambourine."

The answer was "Yes, you do."

I said, "How do I put a gospel song on?"

And I began to play and I have being playing ever since 1994.

When the Lord, once again, gave me a child, I told my husband that I was going to have another baby and this one will live. Now this is six months after I had Joquel. My husband told me, "Maybe it is all in your mind because you just want a baby real bad." I told him I know for a fact, and he still did not believe it. As a matter of fact, no one believed it. Everyone thought I was losing my mind because of the loss of my son. I bought a home test, and it came out positive. My husband was still in disbelief because when I went to the doctor, the test came back negative. They ran tests and said the only thing they see is a cyst on my tubes and scar tissue. There is no way you can get pregnant, but we do have to do surgery immediately.

While in surgery, I can remember dreaming of something very good, but I could not remember what it was. I just remember telling the doctor, while in recovery, that I had a beautiful dream, and I could not stop smiling through all that pain. When I went for my post-op checkup, they told me, "You are expecting a child, and you are ten weeks." The doctor then said, "That would have made you at least three weeks when you had your surgery." They were amazed and called my daughter the miracle baby. My sister even wanted to name her Miracle. Friends and family could not believe it. They would say to me, "I guess God is going to show us what he can do." I have a daughter named Chassade. After her birth, I thanked the Lord for what he has done for me and decided not to try to have any more because I was worried the whole nine months that something was going to happen to her too. I am thankful for what I have and happy with what I have.

My son still visits me from time to time, especially around Christmas because his birthday is December 26, 1993, and he would be eighteen in December 2010. That's why I left the A's here in this book because I know for a fact I did not put it here, and when I counted the A's, there were eighteen of them. My heart feel good because I know this is true.

Today is February 8, 2010, and I am able to sit, write, and think about my son without crying. I thank God for it all. I can feel his presence. It is not that I can see him. It's things like around Christmas my daughter will call me and say, "Momma, Joquel is changing TV channels," and I always tell her, "He is letting you know that he is with you as his little sister." And she gets joy out of it. She is the only child to spoil, and she gets lonely sometimes, and I understand that I could have had more children, but I think she understands why I did not.

Around August 2008, my daughter began to act out having problems in school, talking back and staying in her room a lot. She is fifteen now and has had a good life, but something is wrong when she had her yearly checkup. I talked to the doctor about her, telling him what was going on with her. He decided to send her to talk to another doctor about depression. She had seen the other doctor, and sure enough, she was depressed. Now I was wondering, what was she depressed about? And I was asking myself, was she that lonely? I stopped doing foster care because it was affecting my child. She began to change some when they were here being that she was my child. All the children were treated the same when it came to everyday living. I keep taking her to the doctor. She put her on medication for depression, and she got better, but something is still wrong. She is gaining weight. I am thinking it is because she lay down on her bed every day and sleep, look at TV, and talk on the phone.

Four and a half months have gone by and I decided to take her to the doctor anyway because when I would ask her certain questions, she would say, "No, Mom, this is just fat." I had to know what it was. I was worried by now. It was already four and a half months. I could not get mad at her because I know she is young, but I have a grandson and she named him after her brother, Jocquel. She said, "Momma, your son died, but this is him right here, Momma." I smiled because I know God works in mysterious ways and do good works through her. She has dreams also, and she sees them come to pass. She is learning now to really put all of her faith in God. People are talking, and I am telling her not to worry about what people think or say. I even had several family members say they do not condone in it as though I let my child do this on purpose. Not the truth. She went to visit a friend. They went to a dance at a college for the high school students, not knowing older boys were there, taking advantage of the younger girls. We also had a family member who told her two girls that they could not be around my daughter because she was pregnant. Little did they all know she is a worker for the Lord, started school at three years old at a Christian school, knows the Bible verses so well she can sing them now as I speak.

Both of her girls are having babies. And she has other cousins having babies this year, and a lot of her friends are having babies, and they all are boys, not one of them is a girl. I continue to tell her to hold her head up high, and she is not the first young girl to have a baby just like God allowed me to lose mine. He allowed her to have hers. It was meant to be. We all have things that we have to go through in life. That's why it is best not to point fingers at anyone. I am fifty years old now, old enough to be a grandmother and making the best out of it all. Is this where my son was supposed to be, here as my grandchild and not my son? Only God really knows. Smiles are all over my face. The baby daddy was hitting on my daughter, and I did not know until one day I picked her and the baby up from a friend's house. I noticed that her right eye was swollen. I did not know the baby daddy had her over to his house, hitting on her. That made me sick due to the fact that I had being abused by my first husband. But we are getting through it all. Later, the state must have found out about his age, and they arrested him and charged him with second-degree rape for being with my daughter.

Life has to go on. I make the best of it all because you just can't forget about this handsome little baby boy. He is a child of God also. We all are his children. There is no one person any better than the other. Some people may pretend they are, but they are not. You do not have to be perfect in order to have a personal relationship with the Lord or to serve him. Believe in him. No one on this earth can be just like Jesus. You can only do your best and do not leave him. Those who want to believe it, judge not unless you be judged. The Bible also says, "Let one who has not sinned cast the first stone." Not one of us on this earth can do that if people would tell the truth. My grandbaby is seven months now with five teeth and is trying to walk. He is a happy baby. I love him so much.

\* \* \* \* \*

My daughter is very strong, like her mother, but she does not realize it yet, but she will soon. The depression and mental anger is beating her up. She is still in school, pressing on through the battle, and I know she will come out a winner, and I know her son will be a winner too. We all just have to go through our troubles of this world, but being the winner will require patience, and wait on the Lord and be strong and, by all means, have the faith and hope in God, and he will bring it to pass. After Chassade's first birthday, I was becoming depressed. She had a great birthday party. Barney was there, lots of children, balloons everywhere. She had a great time.

I am realizing that I am not happy. My husband is so disrespectful to me. The name-calling in front of people and behind closed doors were really getting to me. The pushing, slapping, cheating, and threatening ways have driven me to pack some of my things and go. I am disappointed once again, let down by man, but not surprise at all. His voice is so deep when he gets loud with me. It feels like a knife has went through my heart. I refused to get comfortable with that evil spirit that was in him, and by all means, I was not going to let him keep abusing me in front of my daughter. He put me down because I was from the south many days, but that was all right. I just showed him who I was.

By the time Chassade turned nineteen months old, he had use the B word so much. Chassade said it one day, and I knew then and there, no matter how bad, I want this marriage to work. After eight years with him, it was time to go. I began to pack once again, but this time, I did not stop. I did not care about the house, the things that were in it, including him. I did not want it anymore, thinking to myself, I have been married now three times, thinking hard about everything my mother told me after my first marriage-it does not matter how many times you have been married. Do not let man hit on you.

God did not mean for me to be mistreated. He want me happy, so I left Fort Wayne, Indiana, and came back home to stay for good finally. I remarried after two years of being back home, and now I can breathe a little for the first time in years. I can be myself. I can say that all relationships and marriages are going to have their ups and downs, but abuse is not acceptable in my life anymore. I have been married now for thirteen years. Will we stay together? What is God's plan for me? Wherever will he lead me, I will follow. He is my leader.

After I began to write, I wanted to know more about Henry Wells. He is keeping my thoughts occupied a lot these days. I told my sister that I needed to go to Carrollton, Alabama, to see what I can find out about him for my book. A few weeks later, my sister told me that she and a friend had went down there, and someone had her sign a book and for me to go down there to sign it for the history book. It took me awhile, but now that I am getting closer to the end of it, I feel that I need to go even after looking on the computer, TV, and newspapers. I still felt that there is a lot more that I needed to know more because if he is part of my family, I love him the same as the others. And how sad can it get when you do not have some family to care about you if you knew him or not? But knowing about him is enough for me. Something is driving me that way. I have to go, so I tell my mom and some family members that it was time for me to go to Carrollton.

* * * * *

My mother, Laura, Marvin, my first cousin, my husband, Ricky, my grandson, and I went down there. I wasn't afraid. I was so excited and anxious but remained calm. The lady at the front desk greeted us with a smile and was very helpful with helping me locate the person that I needed to talk to. I told her who we were and that we are believed to be family members of Henry Wells. She then called Dora Johnson, but she could not reach her. She was patient with me as for us wanting to see and talk to her. She tried to call her several times but could not reach her. I began to worry that I would not get a chance to visit with him in my own way, but I knew that he knew that I was there. I felt welcomed by him. I was comfortable as though I belonged here. The lady behind the counter gave me Ms. Johnson's phone number and told me to call her later. I said okay, but let her know that we came down.

As I began to leave, I felt that Henry Wells was feeling sad about me leaving, so I quickly turned around, went back into the office, and asked the lady if she could try to call Ms. Johnson one more time. I did not want Henry Wells to be disappointed in me. When she dialed the number, I prayed and she was on the phone. She was at an appointment, and she would be on her way as soon as she was done. What a relief, and the lady in the office recommended some eating place for lunch, and maybe by then Ms. Johnson will be here. We went to a restaurant right there in Carrollton, and the food was good. The only thing I did not like is that they had a side for Alabama fans and a side for— aaaaaaaaaaaaaa aaaaaaaaaaaaaaaaaaaaaaaaaaaaaaaaaaaaaaaaaaaaaaaaaaaaaaaaaaaaa aaa— Auburn fans. There was not enough room for us at the booth that was empty on Alabama side, but I was hungry, so we had to sit at a table on Auburn side in order to have enough room to sit my grandson, who is a small baby, but everything turned out great.

When we got back to the courthouse, I had to use the bathroom, and my mother and the others were sitting in the hall area. I was the only one in the bathroom at the time. I heard noises coming from upstairs as though someone was moving chairs around and dragging chains across the floor. I began to move faster as the sounds got louder. I quickly washed my hands if you know what I mean, so when I came out, I wondered, was that Henry Wells? I went into the office and asked the lady if there was anyone working upstairs, and she said no one had worked up there for years and that the first floor was the only part of the courthouse that was open.

I am excited now and amazed. She then said, "We hear noises all the time, even a little girl crying." I am floored but excited.

After a while, we walked around outside. A lady was selling cakes and pies out front. I bought a pound cake and it was the best. We I could see my mom walking around, looking up at Henry Wells, talking to him. And I did hear her say it's going to be all right. After a while, we went inside. My husband and I decided to walk outside on the other end of the courthouse, being both doors at the courthouse open. We walked outside, stood on the porch, looked around, and read the monuments on the grounds and admired the courthouse. We went back inside. As we began to walk up the hall, Ms. Johnson came through the other door. I said, "There she is." As soon as I said that, the door my husband and I came back in closed shut. By the time I shook Ms. Johnson's hand, we all knew it was Henry Wells. I knew it was him. I knew then that I was doing the right thing. He want us here just like we want him there.

Before we left, I asked my mother to go to the bathroom with me because after the first experience, I will never go to the bathroom down there by myself. This time, my mom, I thought, went into the stall two doors down, and it sounded like the hack of the toilet was moving, and when my mother came out of the stall, she came out of the last stall, which was facing the doorway, and I asked her, "Was that you, Mom?" And she said yes, and then I thought, why would she be messing with the back of a toilet? But she had a warm smile on her face as though she was just trying not to scare me. She took her time and washed her hands, and I did know that she did not enter that stall at all. It was the one next to it. But knowing my mother, she is so powerful with God. She probably knew that I knew what had just happened or she did not realize it. I noticed as I was writing about the restaurant when I got to Alabama and Auburn, the letter A popped up twenty-three times. I know I did not do that, so I will just leave it there anyway.

After we left the courthouse to go back to Tuscaloosa, the clouds began to roll in. A song on the radio came on, and it sang God will open up the windows of heaven and pour you out a blessing, and my mother and I began to sing it at the same time. Everyone else was quiet and listening peacefully, and it began to rain, and the more we sang the song, the harder it rained. It rained so hard we could not see in front of the car, but it seemed as though I knew which way to go, like magic, and in between singing, my mother would say a little prayer, and as we came into Northport, it stopped raining. I knew that the first part of this mission was done.

Later, Ms. Johnson called me, and we set up a time for me to come with other family members to meet the others that are helping retain the courthouse from the bank, and some people and family members are afraid, saying things that they should not say as though I do not know what I am talking about, upsetting my momma so bad that now she will not go back down there. But she know what she is talking about. Same as my uncle Oscar. Before he passed on, I told people about the play that they were going to have down there in April. Some family members were happy. Some asked about money. One said that I took over her project. In fact, I am the one who is writing this book. She talked about me to other family members and friends, but *it does not matter*. Whatever God has for me to do, I will do it.

People tried to turn my daughter against me, but she is old enough now to know what is true and what is not and who is real and who is not for real, she calls it, and some people don't know this is pertaining to my mother's side of the family, not my father's. Through it all, I am encouraged by Ms. Johnson to come back down. This time, the man from the bank met me. Ricky, Marvin and my grandbaby rode down one day and took him to the family cemetery, and I walked him out there to see all the Wells' graves. Lo and behold, he ran up on a Burkhaulter, which is the last name of the man who ran with Henry Wells back when the courthouse was burned down. He was so surprised. There were other old graves with only stones and no marker that were hundreds of years old. Is Henry here? As of right now, no one knows where he is. There is a connection with Henry Wells and the Burkhaulter. I never would have put it together if it had not been for Ms. Johnson being so caring and wanting to get the truth out, just as I do and the other family members. And I feel that if I had been someone else to go after the truth, other family members would believe them. Will they believe me now? Some will and some will just brush me off and cannot stand to hear the real truth. I just thank God for what he has done. I think back when I first went down there and Ms. Johnson was telling me about the play, and here I come looking for the truth.

It is hard to explain important things to people when they only think about money. Some asked me, "Are we going to get some money?" I just tell them no. I can explain all I want. They will not listen to the truth and will not realize this is not about getting some money. It is about being there for your family and knowing the truth, and they need to also know that the courthouse did not belong to Henry Wells. That's where he went to jail. The courthouse belongs to the city of Carrollton, and if they are having a play to help repair old problems in the building, then I think that is great. Everything needs repairs, even our bodies, and that will help preserve Henry Wells's face in the window. I would not want it torn down as though he was nothing. My mother is excited about me going to the play. Some people think they should not have to pay. Why not? They pay to go see other plays but do not want to pay to see one of your family member's? I see now why they have the saying money is the root of all evil. Either way, they had a sell out for all four nights— April 15, 16, 17, and 18.

Whoever did not get their tickets will not be going.

Today is April 14, 2010. The play starts tomorrow night at seven o'clock in the evening. I will be going on Saturday. I just called my friend Jonnie to ask her how to spell several words, and as she spelled *Auburn* for me, more A's popped up on the screen, and I am so excited. I am laughing and she is saying, "What?" I told her I would let her read about it, but I do know I did not put all those A's up there. I have to stop now. I am getting emotional. Now I had to exhale. I feel like I want to cry, but I know I am strong. But let me remind you that there is nothing wrong with crying if you know what you are crying for. Is it joy or happiness? I will always thank Ms. Johnson for giving me the inspiration and encouragement to continue on my mission. She told me one day that I would cry, laugh, be sad, and happy. Now I am able to finish with all the emotions involved. We all just got to keep it real at all times. Thank God I am able to stand in the gap for my mother. God and I were able to be with my mom during her cancer treatments. I am moving to another location, and I love it. The devil is the only one that is mad. I have been bit by a poisonous spider in three places, both on the legs around my knees and on my upper arm, swelling with redness and pain, so I got to the Crimson Urgent Care, which is on the next street over. I was feeling dizzy but I made it. I just thank God that it did not bite my daughter, grandson, or my husband. I took that I am still going to do what God has for me to do. The devil is so mad, but he needed to understand that he got to come through God to get to me. Big, tall, small, round, or fat, I will not be afraid.

**DESCENDANTS OF HENRY WELLS GATHER INFORMATION FOR BOOK**

Descendants of the late Henry Wells, who legend says is the Face in the Window [at] the Pickens County Courthouse, visited the county last week to gather information [for] a book. Brenda Turner of Tuscaloosa, second from right, shown with her husba[nd] Richard, right, holds a picture of Henry Wells' brother and is going to be the author [of] her autobiography entitled "Missing Pieces: The Truth." Mrs. Turner's mother, Lau[ra] Hurst Smith, second from left, is the daughter of the late Oredeal Wells Hurst who w[as] the daughter of Oscar Wells who was the son of Clifford Wells, who is believed to [be] the brother of Henry Wells. At left is Marvin Hurst, grandson of Oredeal Hurst.

# FAMED FACE-IN-THE-WINDOW
# OF PICKENS COUNTY COURTHOUSE

One of the first things a visitor hears about in Pickens County is "The Face In The Window," th supposed image of a jailed black man impressed on an upper window of the Pickens Count Courthouse at Carrollton.

Local historians claim that the image belonged to one Henry Wells, who was arrested in 187 for burning the old Carrollton Courthouse two years earlier. As the story goes, when the badl wounded fugitive was dragged back into town, an outraged mob had formed to seek quic vengeance for the fire and other crimes Henry had reportedly committed.

Fearing for Henry's life, local lawmen hid him in the garret of the new courthouse. While th angry mob smoldered below, an electrical storm crackled through the area. Just as a jagged spea of lightning ripped the sky, Henry looked down in terror--his face instantly, and indelibly, printed o the window, looking for all the world like a photo negative.

This all sounds like some yarn-spinner's foolishness until you stand in Carrollton's town squar at high noon and look up to see the ghostly image staring down at you. Local chill seekers eve claim on stormy nights, the wind makes weird noises around the towering courthouse eaves, an as lightning licks across the boiling black sky, Henry Wells can be seen peering sorrowfully throug the garret window.

Of course, there is much more to the history of Pickens County than the story of an unhapp ghost. The county was founded in 1820 and named after Gen. Andrew Pickens.

Perhaps one of the most significant developments from the meshing of Picken's past and pres ent has come in the area of human relations. There is tangible contrast between the tense atmos phere of the Reconstruction period and the productive attitude of racial cooperation and accommo dation which exists today.

# UNKNOWN

My heart weeps, but my soul is happy. It is Saturday, April 17, 2010. We are getting ready to go to the play down at the courthouse in Carrollton, Alabama. I am feeling better now from the spider bites, and I am ready to go. After we arrived, I realized that there were no babies or children. My grandson was not able to go into the play, so therefore, we had to decide who would go in with me-either my daughter, Chassade, or my husband, Ricky. He agreed to let Chassade go in, being that was her uncle and all. So we were just out of a $20 ticket. I still kept my cool until I had seen the acton that played Henry Wells get out of a sheriff's car and was escorted by the actor that play the sheriff. As they walked up to the courthouse, it was then that I went back into the pass. Just seeing it reenacted seems so real as though I was there actually, looking at this. By the time I reached the last step, the tears stopped. Tears began to roll down my cheeks uncontrollably. They would not stop until I walked up the stairs. The tears stopped after I reached the last step. We went in and sit down.

Ms. Johnson, my daughter, and I did get a front row seat being that we were in the line at the front, walking in behind Barry Bradford in front of the line, knowing that he took out the time to put this play together. It was a sellout.

We saved a seat for Ms. Johnson. She was busy making sure everything was going right. I am so excited to see this play, knowing that it was going to reveal the truth about Henry Wells. The name of the play is *The Face in the Courthouse Window*. As the play began, I felt so sad, and there were other times during the play I would cry and laugh. I felt happiness, and by the end of the play, I felt peace. My daughter was very pleased to know the truth, finally knowing that he didn't rape anyone, and all the untrue stories have been defeated. Barry did a great job doing his research. The First National Bank of Central Alabama Preservation Foundation and the tourism association played a big role in this presentation. The cast was Willie William as Henry Wells; Angela Fraier as Caroline Wells, who was Henry's wife; Keven Long as Bill Burkhaulter, who was with Henry when he was on the run; Jerrell Bowden as Mose Ligon, who ran with Henry also; George Thagard as Sheriff James Gates; John Brandon as Dr. Sam Hill; Jake Hougaboom as John Hunnicutand. They had other characters, such as Westcott as Gilliam, Lynn Holmes E. B., David Abston as Lem.

As we know Barry Bradford did the playwright, Sara Norris did the directing, Frank Duren did the sounds, John Hisay did the lights, Bobby Horton did the music, and Michelle Mumtifering and Nick Shabel were stage managers. My mother, Laura Hurst Smith, my uncle Robert, my brother Billy, or should I say Bishop Billy Hurst, and other family members would all like to thank everyone who had a part in this historical event. As you may know, Ricky and my grandson stayed downstairs until the play was over. As I was walking to the car, my cousin hit my mind, thinking about how she lied and told Ricky to bring my grandson to Gordo and that she would keep him. And when he got there, my aunt told him that she had left. I knew the people do not care about other people's feelings, only their own, but everything turned out okay. They have the gift shop open, band playing music outside. I fill complete now, and now my child knows the truth for herself. She can teach her son about this, and they will not have to live thinking the worse about uncle Henry. He was not perfect either, but he was a good man, and he had Jesus and he really loved his family.

Every year in April, they will put on this play just have to go to the First National Bank of Tuscaloosa, Alabama, or any First National Bank. I meet a lot of people, and Ms. Johnson made sure that she introduces me to everyone. She had me stand before the play began. At the end of the play, tears began to roll down my face, stronger than before, uncontrollably. I walked over to Barry and gave him a big hug and then walked over to Ms. Johnson and gave her a big hug. I felt a sense of relief and as though I was feeling what my uncle was feeling. I got it together and took pictures with Willie, and it seems as though it was Henry Wells himself. I feel part of him more so than ever. I do know that great care was taken to be as accurate as possible; pieces are coming together. I knew it was going to be a good play when I saw Senator Phil Poole come into the door (smile).

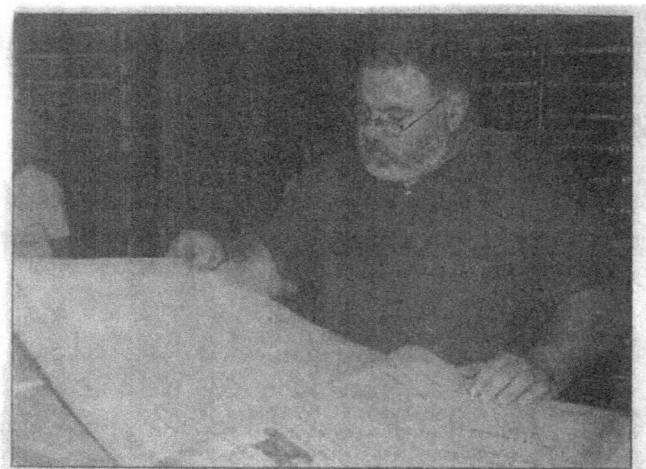

BARRY BRADFORD LOOKS THROUGH AN OLD WEST ALABAMIAN
NEWSPAPER TO FIND OUT DETAILS ABOUT THE HENRY WELLS LEGEND

# Play could help save infamous Pickens County courthouse

## Play based on legend to be performed in courthouse

By Mark Hughes Cobb
Staff Writer

A new play based on the legend of Henry Wells, who allegedly torched the Pickens County Courthouse in 1876, may ironically help save the replacement building where Wells' haunted face is said to be burned by lightning into a garret window.

"When you say you're from Pickens County, people either say 'Well, that's where my hunting club is' or 'That's where the face in the window is,'" said Leon Manning, senior vice-president of First National Bank of Central Alabama, which is producing the play. "It's clearly an asset we could build up."

Proceeds from the play "The Face in the Courthouse Window," which will see its debut produc-

Playwright Barry Bradford, left, has completed "The Face in the Courthouse Window." Sarah Norris will direct the debut production.

tion April 15-18, will go to the Pickens County Courthouse Preservation Committee.

Manning looked to Monroeville, which annually performs "To Kill a Mockingbird" in and around the Monroe County Courthouse, Harper Lee's model for her novel's Maycomb Courthouse. That show is not only a tourist draw for Monroeville, but it has toured internationally and played at the Kennedy Center in Washington, D.C.

Wells' story shares elements with Lee's tale, including a small Alabama town and its central courthouse, an incensed white population and a hated black antagonist.

But the Carrollton tale has the additional virtues of being at least partly true and, as legend

SEE PLAY | 9E

SEE PLAY | 9E

Tuscaloosa News

From left, Willie Williams, Jerrell Bowden and Kevin Long rehearse a scene from "The Face in the Courthouse Window" at the Pickens County Courthouse in Carrollton on Saturday. The play runs April 15-18, and all proceeds benefit the restoration of the courthouse.

# Courthouse theater

## Carrollton hosts play to benefit restoration of historic building

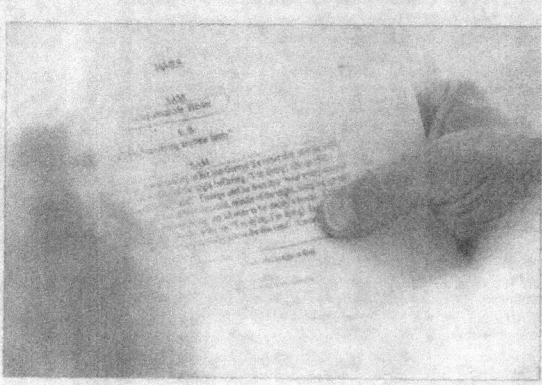

John Brandon reads over a scene from "The Face in the Courthouse Window" during a rehearsal on Saturday.

Tuscaloosa News

STAFF FILE PHOTO

The play "The Face in the Courthouse Window" will be performed at the Pickens County Courthouse April 15-18. The courthouse is at the intersection of Highways 86 and 17. Proceeds from the $20 tickets will help the courthouse's restoration.

The legend goes that Wells was caught in Fairfield by a Sheriff Gates, who tried to protect Wells from a furious lynch mob by stashing him in the courthouse attic. As the crowd roared and threatened below, Wells protested his innocence. According to Windham, he declared, "If you kill me, I am going to haunt you for the rest of your lives."

Lightning struck.

What happened then is open to interpretation.

Again, factually, Wells died that night, shot to death trying to flee incarceration.

The next day, people began seeing what appeared to be Wells' visage, twisted into a grimace of terror, etched into the glass where he'd faced the mob. What the image might be, it's still visible today, moreso in certain lights and times of day than others. It's become such a draw that Carrollton installed a reflective sign on the brick facing next to the window, pointing to the pane where the "face" appears. A set of mounted binoculars are positioned across the

Bradford, who lives in Hammond, La., showed Manning the rest of the play committee a script a few weeks ago, and the committee made a few small suggestions. The final approved script is now ready, and Sarah Norris, a Huntsville native and University of Alabama graduate who came back to town last year to direct "The Foreigner" for Theatre Tuscaloosa, has taken the reins. Auditions will be held Jan. 5 at Shelton State's Bean-Brown Theatre in Tuscaloosa, and Jan. 7 in at the courthouse in Carrollton.

Though he knows the truth may not be as exciting as the legend, Bradford stuck as closely as possible to the facts, creating motives and filling in story details where they weren't available.

"We start near the end, actually, and go back. The play opens with Henry Wells in custody

Dora Johnson is president of the Pickens County Courthouse Preservation Committee.

we start with his confession, then go back to tell the events leading to that point," he said.

The conflicts aren't just of the crime-and-punishment sort, but from obvious tensions of Reconstruction, when the white community struggled to rebuild as an emerging black ex-slave class sought to create its place in the world.

"It's a conflict that sort of illustrates the times," Bradford said.

"I was very careful to portray the white community in an honest light, without bashing either one. The play focuses on Henry Wells as a member of that community, trying to assert itself, its new-found voting and civil rights.

"But it's also honest in the sense that we don't try to paint Henry Wells as a saint. Based on what I've seen in the record, he was a thief, he did rob from

stores, he did burn down some stores. He was accused, and apparently rightly so, of burning down the courthouse."

Even with its adherence to fact, the play builds to the lightning strike, with all its supernatural suggestiveness. That climactic moment is one of the chief concerns for Norris, who's just received the script. It's not a large-budget production, and the courthouse is not a theater that can be easily manipulated, so how to make such a moment work is her early focus, along with creating character breakdowns for auditions. But she's thrilled with the chance to direct it, she said, and very happy with the complexity of Bradford's script.

"There's a lot of back story for Henry: why he did the crimes, how the crimes started, and taking us through a couple of those first robberies," said Norris, who lives in New York City. "It gives his take of why he's robbing: his friends are robbing for different reasons. Then you have his wife, who wants him to stop, give everything back. But he's doing it to feed his family, so he's not just an ordinary criminal."

What happens after the lightning strike, and the creation of the "face," is left open-ended.

"It leaves there where you can leave debating," Norris said. "It doesn't say 'This was the answer.' It leaves it up to the audience to talk about and discuss, which I think is cool."

Bradford said he couldn't get into the ghost-story elements without veering too far from established facts.

"We don't really get into the spooky stuff, although obviously there's a whole realm of ghost stories connected with Henry Wells in the courthouse," he said.

After a short pause, he added, "I actually had a couple of weird things happen to me," laughing, "that kind of made me think twice."

The first was when he was visiting the courthouse, taking reference photographs. His camera worked fine throughout

the building, until he climbed to the garret room.

"I could not get my camera to take a picture up there," he said. "It would just turn off when I climbed up there. That was very strange."

Later, he met with Manning at a Shell station in nearby Reform and began talking about how the flash of lightning would strike and the face would appear.

"I was talking about how to make the flash happen, and the sound of thunder, and literally the instant I finished saying the sentence, a transformer across the street exploded. It blew up. There was a tremendous, huge bang; it got white hot, so bright you couldn't look at it. All the power on the street went out," he said.

Obviously, you can't recreate that kind of effect on a limited budget. So he kept the script intentionally light of stage direction, knowing the debut performance, at least, will be in the courthouse rather than a traditional theater, which has lighting, sound and other effects.

"He wrote it where you could do it anywhere," Norris said. "He kept things simple, knowing we're not going to have lavish sets. It's about the characters, about the story, not much about the spectacle. I left a lot of room to play with."

Manning hopes the play will become an annual draw, like Monroeville's "Mockingbird." They plan to make the debut run a big deal, with Windham scheduled to attend opening night, and the 5th Alabama Infantry Regimental Band performing. Bobby Horton, a former Three on a String band member whose work has been heard on Ken Burns' Civil War and baseball documentaries, is composing the score.

Tickets are already beginning to sell, Manning said. The courthouse, at the intersection of Highways 86 and 17, will seat 160 each for four performances at 7 p.m. April 15-17 and 2 p.m. April 18. For tickets and other information, see www.courthousewindow.com.

# FAMILY

After seeing the play, I know my family on the Wells side were all good people and love their family. As of today, the love still goes on, and I know this is what brought me through, with God's help, of course. Some of us are good people but have some other ways that they probably got from the other side of their family, like some of the younger generation. Now as far as my mom and her brothers and sisters, they are the most loving people in the world, kind, sweet, and will be there when you need them, no questions asked and that's with everything. And that is why it is hard to be around negative people. I learned everything from them, starting from Henry. We all may not be perfect people, but we have a lot of love in our hearts and will help anyone if we can. I'm glad to say that I cannot think of anything bad that all eight my mother siblings ever did to me, and I'm fifty *years* of age now.

Now there's a difference with my father's people. Some of them will not even give you a ride home, and they can live four doors down from your house and they will say I'm not going that way. And you have some that will not feed you, and if they do, they talk about it. For instance, strangers can come in and they will feed them, but if family members are hungry, they talk about it and tell lies and tell other people you tried to eat up all their food. Coldhearted. And I detect jealousy when it comes to me buying. I don't care. I know I am loved, thanks to the Wells and Hurst families. But don't get me wrong, not all of them are like that, but they know who they are. Can't stand to see me coming, may get a hung and may not. I've learn to live with it and cherish the ones that do love or care for me. I am done crying and hurting for what people do to me. I give them to Jesus once and for all, and that goes for everyone who have lied on me, talked about me, envied me, mistreated me, called me names, and the ones that just do not like me because I am me and tried to disrespect my home where there should be peace. The ones that disrespect me because they think I am one way, but I am not, and due to all the harsh lies, instead of getting to know me for themselves, they try to turn people against me for no reason at all.I think they call that hating.

The true people in my life know who they are even if I do not see them, only a few times a year. Real love never goes away. It is something that you feel, not what you see. Family members are leaving this world now. My uncle passed on, who is my father's brother, on December 18. We buried him, and the only thing people were thinking about is money and who is going to sit in front of who just because I took care of him in his last days. It was to the point where the lies about me were flowing from north to south and from south to north. No one was really totally concerned about him but me and a few others. They know who they are. Well, I got beyond that, had him a nice home going, I call it, overlooked the ones that did not speak, had my sister sing because I just could not get up there. I was so hurt about his passing being that the doctor told me that my uncle was going to pass on because he was malnourished. And I was noting that he was in the nursing home. At the time, he checked himself into the nursing home. I believe he did not want all that stress on me, and I had my restaurant at the Brenda's Hometown Deli, so one day, when I got home, my husband told me that he got a call that he had checked himself into the nursing home. He had bed sores. He was diagnosed with Alzheimer's disease. I would always go to the nursing home to see him and made a lot of complaints. No one listened. They even took his money. I give them to Jesus also. The dreams are still coming true. I tell my mother all of my dreams, so one morning, I called her and told her that I had dreams about a pair of cuff links and that they were silver. A few weeks later, my uncle Hurman, who is one of my mother's brothers, passed on October 30, 2010. He was born on October 4, 1943. He was sixty-seven years old. I cannot think of one thing wrong that he has ever done to me. His daughter asked me if I wanted to do a poem, and this is the first poem I have ever written and this is what came from my heart.

# My Uncle

Roses are red and violets are blue.
Everyone should want an uncle just
like you because you had always seen me through.
When I cried, it was you, when I had troubles,
it was you, so thank you very much for helping
my wishes come true, and that is just one of the
reasons that God loves you, so I don't worry because
you have been made new. God blessed you because you
were true that's why I thank God for having an uncle
just like you, and I will always love you.

PS:
And praying one day I will be where you are too.

# TRIP TO ORLANDO FLORIDA

A re we listening? Are we really trying to change? I hope so. After seeing Jesus on the side of the expressway, standing there draped the way it was in the Bible days, wearing sandals with straps up his leg and me figuring out later that there is no room there for anyone to stand. This confirmed what I believe in the Lord. In 1997, when I took a trip to Orlando, Florida, I am so fearful of flying on a plane. Satan had me on edge. My heart was racing, but after we went over the Gulf of Mexico, coming out of New Orleans, where we had a layover, after all this, I could not take anymore of my first time on a plane. After we got higher into the clouds, I looked out of the window to my right and saw beautiful colors shining so brightly. I took a picture of it, and others had seen it too, but there was no reaction from anyone but me. After I got home, I did not *remember* taking the picture until after I got the film developed, and then everything came back to me. I did not believe what I had seen. It was the image of Jesus, and I went to sleep. When I woke up, we were in Florida. The picture I took looked like Jesus with his arm open and up in the left upper corner looked like Satan upset because God stepped in. Are we listening? Can we see it? Are we trying to change?

I have seen a lot, and I do not mind sharing these things with anyone else. Some people may not like me because I have my own opinion about life. What's the difference? Everyone has a right to their own opinion. What is is, what is not is not. Now I can relate with reality and face the truth. I am not the one that will spill my guts, but I will give you enough choice. I feel that we need to free ourselves from fear. I don't think that God would mind if we would just relax and have confidence in him and try to accept what comes and accept what goes, then comes a peace of mind. I have learned not to get worry in doing well and that he will always see us through. I also have learned that lack of knowledge will destroy you, and that it is easier to listen and learn.

I had the opportunity to visit with my aunt Vert Cheatum Washington in the Reform Alabama Nursing Home. At 103 years old, she gave me insight on my life, and now I know who I am and expt who I am and proud of who I am. Knowing that her mother was white and her father was an Indian named Dully Cheatum and Aunt Vert is my great-grandmother Alzalee Cheatum Wells's sister, that made me feel proud. My grandmother Ora Deal Wells Hurst is Alzalee's daughter. And then my mother Laura Lee Hurst Smith is Ora Deal's daughter, and I am Laura's baby daughter, Brenda Sue, they call me, and my grandmother Ora Deal named me when I was born. I was taught well. It is a privilege to come from people that is great and royal. What an honor. I can move on now and cherish these awesome encounters and the people that I admire and has learned a lot of inspirational things from over the years by way of TV and radio and books. These are Pastor T. D. Jake, Maya Angelou, Juanita Bynum, Oprah Winfrey, and Michael Jackson. No, Michael is not a preacher, but let's admit he was a great performer. My mother, Henry Wells, and God are very pleased with the mission I am on. The rest does not matter. My uncle Robert has given me information that is very viable and filled in a lot of pieces, and I am so grateful. He is my last living uncle on my mother's side, and I thank God for him. It is good to know the name of the Indian tribe that we came from on my grandmother Ora Deal Hurst's mother side of the family. I was told what the name of the tribe that we come from is Saint Augustine, and that was told to my family from the time they were children. As for as the spelling, it could have been spelled differently. We just spelled it the way it sounds. Either way, I am pleased with my search for the missing pieces.

# FAMILY

My first encounter with a Cheatum was back in the 1960s, and that was Coach Earl Wilson Cheatum at Riverside High School in Northport, Alabama. He taught summer programs for the younger children in the neighborhood. I can remember after going outside for the daily activities, Coach Cheatum would pass out cold milk to all the children. As the delivery man brings it into the classroom, you could hear the glass bottles that they came in clicking together. He was very kind and an excellent coach. Now this is about forty-one years later, and I went to my doctor, Paremsetty, for an appointment, and I see someone that looked familiar to me, but I did not say anything because I wasn't sure until Stacy called his name, and when I heard the name Cheatum, I forgot the first name because Cheatum rang a bell, but before he left my presence, he asked me, "Where do I know you *from?*" I asked him if his name was Robert Cheatum, and he said yes. I told him he was my cousin. That confirmed the unity that we have as a family. You just know. So later, I called my uncle Robert, and he told me that he was Coach Cheatum's son. We did not get a chance to discuss anything about the family, and I don't know if I will ever see him again, but I do know that meeting was for a reason.

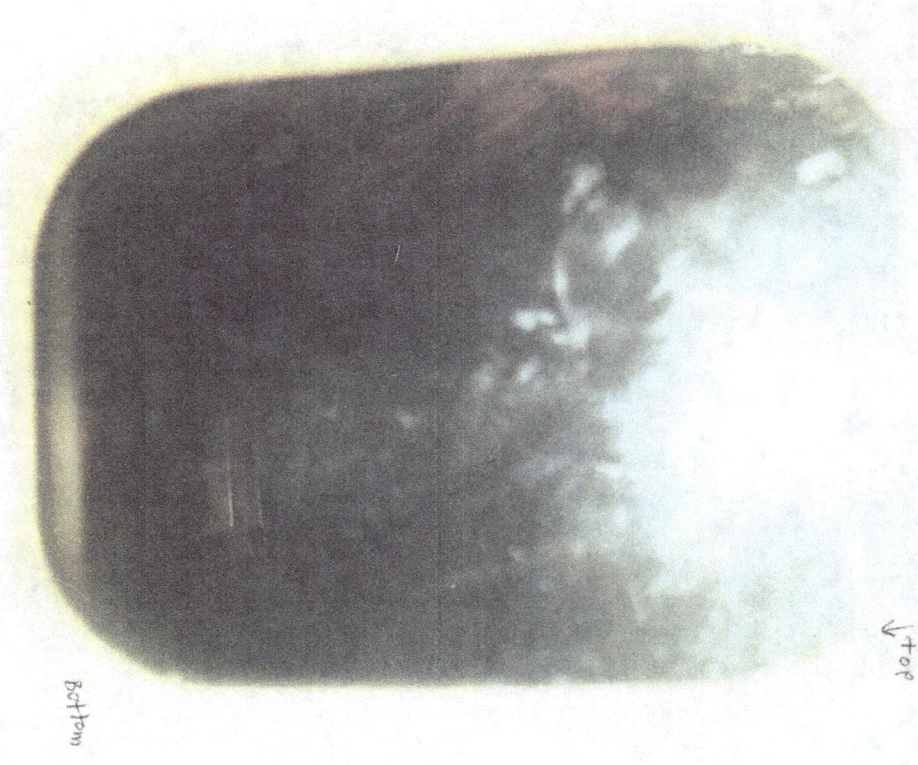

Bottom

↖ top

Picture taken at night while Flying to Florida
From inside the plain Emege of "Jesus"

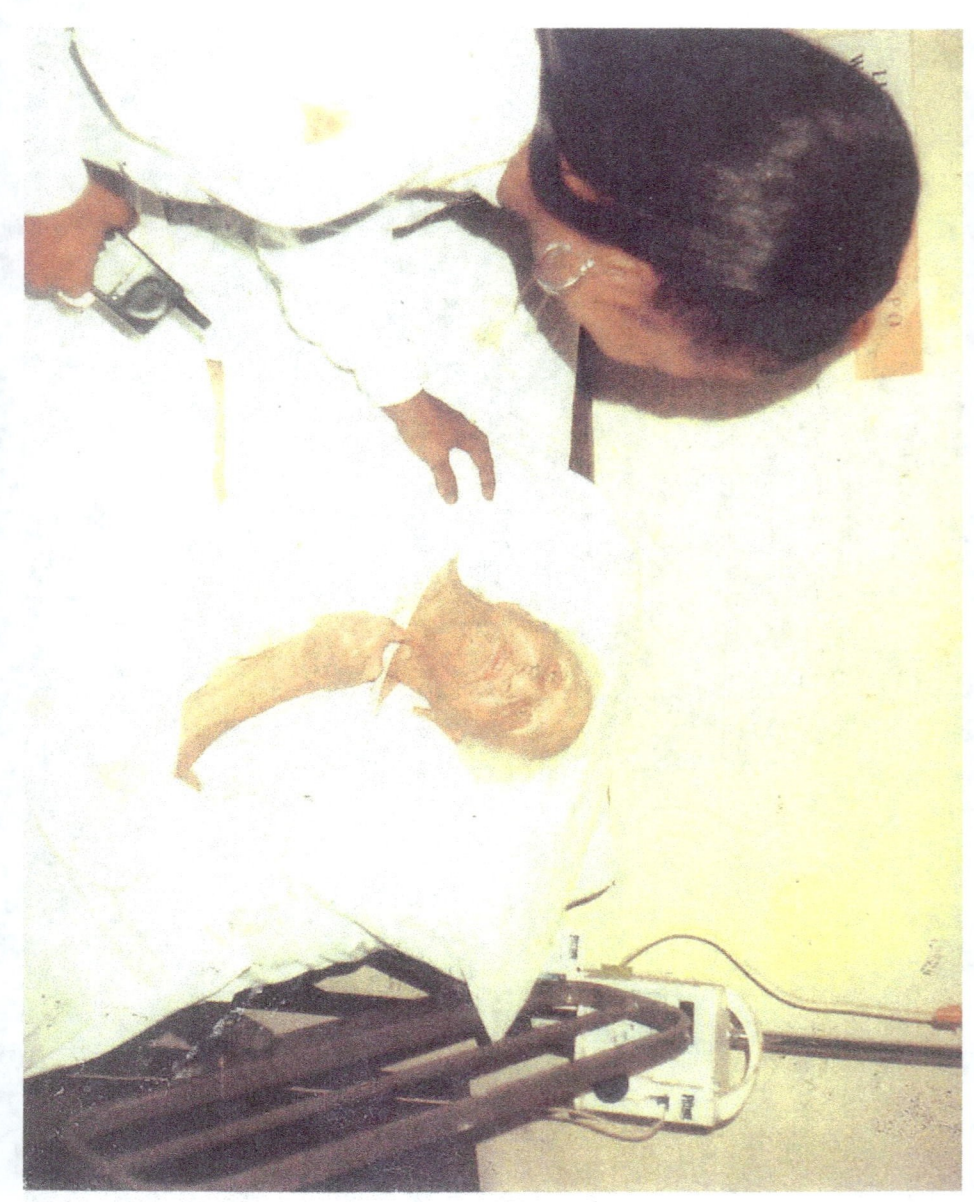

Alzalee Sister
my Aunt Vert Cheatum wells Washington
Dolly Cheatum daughter

Great Grandmother – AlzaLee Cheatum Wells
AlzaLee Well'sisCheatum Dolly
Daughter

# CHURCH

I t is sad, but it is true that, sometimes, in some families, it takes death to really bring them together and to know that a family that prays together stays together. That's the answer to the separations in some families. I hope we all know the importance of sticking together through it all and giving love as we should do and understanding that we all are different. And know there is a reason for all things and know our purpose here on this earth. And always remember that in order to grow stronger and to be something, you got to go through something. I am still having dreams, and for the last seven years, I hear a sound in my right ear that sounds like a horn blowing. Sometimes, it blows softly, and I feel a sense of love and peace, and sometimes, I feel that something is going to happen because every time the horn blows loud, someone I know will die or some type of trouble will come. I can't pinpoint what it is, so I just pray to the Lord to have mercy on whatever it may be.

At first I thought something was going wrong with my hearing or maybe it was my sinus acting up. I tried everything that I could think of to do to fix the problems, like checking my hearing and taking sinus medication.

I only can hear the horn in my right ear, so I switched side of the bed, thinking maybe the sound is coming from the house, but none of these things was the answer, so now I just accept it and know that I cannot stop it, and I know it comes from Jesus. He always gives me a warning. And through it all, I will not be ashamed of the wrong that people have done to me. I did nothing wrong. I will not feel guilty for seeking my peace, love, joy, and happiness that God has given to me. Thank you, Jesus, for answering my prayers and keeping me here on this earth long enough for this special journey.

My legs are bothering me now from the accidents that I had back when I was a little girl. I had to let the restaurant go. I can't work on my feet like I used to, but I thank God for the years that he gave me to work, and I will not be ashamed of the mistakes that I have made or be ashamed of the mistakes that people have made to me, not forgetting being lied on, talked about, mistreated, and not being ashamed for knowing who my love is.

I am back in the choir now at New Zion Baptist Church in Northport, Alabama, singing and playing my tambourine for Jesus. This is where he wants me now, and I know this is for a reason, a special reason. I am thanking God for the positivity, the motivation, the patience, and all that spiritual guidance that he has given to me, and always remembering that sometimes the ones that are the closest to you are the furthest from you and the ones that are the furthest from you are the closest to you. Now I am thanking God for the ones that do understand me, and I can proudly say that I will not turn my back on my family and friends, and I am grateful for the wonderful doctors that I have, who play a great part in my life when it comes down to my health. Another thing I have learned is that it is important to forgive because it will heal and to accept the things that I can change and to accept the things that I cannot change. This brings you peace. I will always tell the truth that brings relief. The end. (Date January 11, 2011)

Grandpa Cliff Wells
Henry Wells brother

Cliff Wells
and his son          Gordo, Al
Oscar Wells My mother's Grandfather

Henry Wells In the window

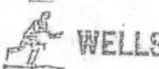

Shrewsbury, Mass.
G. T. Shaw

30 Jan, 1878 P. 2

## A Stormy Debate in the Senate.

WASHINGTON, Jan. 22.—In the Senate, after the morning hour, Messrs. Hamlin and Blaine presented the statue of Wm. King, contributed by the State of Maine to the National Statuary Hall at the capitol. It contains remarks reviewing the services of King. Mr. Blaine commented on the feeling of the people of Massachusetts towards those of Maine, before the latter was a state and while it was a part of Massachusetts, and alluded to Boston as constituting then, even more than now, the governing power in Massachusetts. He said finally that the people of Maine formed a separate state, and they were indebted for their success to the fear in the minds of the governing political party of Massachusetts that their success would be endangered, if Maine should continue to be an integral portion of the State. He commented severely on the action of the people of Massachusetts and commended the course of William King in opposing them. The Massachusetts Senators, Messrs. Dawes and Hoar, attacked the Maine Senator, and the former challenged him to mention an instance when Massachusetts ever was guilty of an unpatriotic act. Mr. Blaine immediately replied that she was opposed to the war of 1812, and refused to let her troops go out of the State. The whole affair was intensely enjoyed by the Democratic side of the Chamber, and when the Senator from Maine and the Massachusetts Senators were assailing each other with some feeling, a voice on the Democratic side was heard to exclaim, "Well, this is rich." Mr. Blaine was particularly severe on the course of Massachusetts during the war of 1812, and his recital of historical facts was not relished by the Senator from that State.

Illustrative of the character of the senatorial fight between Blaine and ...

## HERE HE IS!

## HENRY WELLS,

### The Notorious Negro Robber and House Burner, Captured and Lodged in Jail.

We shift the form to make room for the glad tidings of the capture of the notorious outlaw, Henry Wells. He was arrested yesterday morning on the plantation of Bill McConner, near Fairfield. Ala., by Messrs. H. C. and W. B. Sawls. After his arrest he made a desperate effort to get away, but two well directed pistol shots brought him to his senses. We understand he acknowledges the "corn"— that he confesses to burning the court-house of our county. He was identified by our young friend, B. B. Cohen, formerly of this place, but who is now clerking for Mr. Windham, near the plantation where this negro has been employed since last fall. Henry Wells and Bill Buckhalter are now confined in our jail.

### "When Shall the End Be?"

On last Sabbath, in Chicago, in the absence of Rev. Mrs. Mansfield, her husband, Rev. Mr. Mansfield, filled the pulpit for her. His subject seems to have been earthquakes, as one of the signs of the second coming of Christ. We make the following extracts from his sermon, as reported in the Chicago Tribune:

Mr. Mansfield took up a small scrap...

## TURKEY ACCEPTS THE TERMS.

### A War Indemnity of £20,000,000 to be Demanded.

### The Terms of Russia's Proposals to the Vanquished Ottomans.

LONDON, January 25.—Reuter has the following from Constantinople, under to-day's date: "The Porte having yesterday accepted the Russian conditions, peace may be considered as virtually concluded. The Russian conditions are not yet officially known here, but it appears certain that they greatly exceed the Conference programme, and stipulate both for territorial concessions and the payment of a war indemnity."

The Daily Telegraph, in its second edition, prints the following from Constantinople: "The Turkish delegates have been ordered to sign the peace preliminaries. An armistice will probably be concluded to-day. The peace conditions are stated, on excellent authority, to include the following: Servia to be independent, without compensation. Montenegro to receive Antivari, Niesic and Spez, and a portion of the territory bordering on Lake Scutari; Russia to hold Batoum, Kars and Erzeroum, until a war indemnity of twenty million pounds is paid; the Dardanelles to be opened to the Russian men of war; Bulgarian autonomy to be conceded rather on the principles of the Lebanon, than on the plan of the Constantinople Conference, and Turkey to nominate a Christian Governor for a long term of years subject to ratification by the Powers; Bulgaria not to be understood to include Thrace, but only to extend to the line of the Balkans; part of the Russian army to embark at Constantinople for their return home, and the final treaty of peace to be signed at Constantinople by the Grand Duke Nicholas. This arrangement will satisfy the Russian...

# Legendary face mellows with storytelling

By John Carmichael
Dec. 13, 2002

Visitors to Carrollton who stand on the north side of Pickens County's courthouse and gaze at an attic window might see the image of a face staring back from one of the panes. If they stand around long enough they will likely hear one of the town's residents relate a version of the "face in the window" legend.

Preservationists helped renovate Pickens County's courthouse, site of the legendary "face in the window." (Photo by Brandon Pierce)

According to the "official" account, promoted by the Pickens County Courthouse Preservation Committee, the story began in 1876, when an arsonist burned down the previous courthouse. Two years later Henry Wells, a suspect in the crime, was arrested after being shot by his pursuers. He died in jail soon afterward.

Issues of the West Alabamian from the time report that the courthouse was "consumed" by the fire in two hours and the probate court records were destroyed. "It is indeed a calamity upon our county," the newspaper report said. It estimated the new courthouse would cost around $20,000.

The courthouse, which had been rebuilt after Union soldiers burned down an earlier version during the Civil War, "was a credit to the county," the paper said. The paper also speculated that the 1876 fire was "unquestionably the work of an incendiary. It took fire in several places about the same time."

Two years later, a story appeared in the West Alabamian with the headline "HERE HE IS! HENRY WELLS, The Notorious Negro Robber and House Burner, Captured and Lodged in Jail." Wells had been arrested on a plantation in Fairfield and had tried to escape. His pursuers, H.C. and W.B. Sawls, shot him twice and hauled him to Carrollton. Bill Burkhalter, accused of helping Wells in the arson, had already been caught and was being held in town.

The next week's issue of the paper printed Wells' deathbed confession. The gunshot wounds had proved fatal, but before he died Wells admitted that he and Burkhalter had been stealing from various stores in Pickens County on the night of the 1876 fire.

According to the newspaper's report, Burkhalter believed the safe in the probate office held a large amount of money, so the men broke into the courthouse. Unable to open the safe, they took tobacco and "some little brass things" from the building. Wells left a candle near some papers that eventually caught fire.

The newspaper's account, however, does not verify the rest of the legend.

Modern versions of the story claim Wells was brought to Carrollton under the threat of a lynch mob. To protect their suspect from the mob, authorities hid Wells in the attic of the newly rebuilt courthouse. The mob gathered under the attic's window while Wells watched with terror. An electrical storm erupted and a bolt of lightning struck across the street from the courthouse square. The flash etched Wells' frightened image in the window pane, where it can still be seen today.

# Handcuffs Reportedly Worn By Henry Wells

hese old handcuffs are ned by a man in Aliceville brought them to us with a y that these are the dcuffs that brought Henry lls, to Carrollton the night was struck by lightening in Pickens County Courthouse. course, everyone already vs the rest of that story. ther these actually are the handcuffs that brought Henry Wells in is a matter of question for sure. But also for sure is the fact that they are indeed very old. The owner has contacted several law enforcement agencies and he reports that not a single officer has ever seen a pair like them.

Consisting of solid iron, they are hinged on one end and have a screw that closes the other end. The key shown releases and tightens that screw. If the handcuffs look too small to you, you should try putting them on. If a criminal was held by them he had no means of escape. The owner of the handcuffs says that they were passed down to him through his family.

... ... ... William, the popular Alabama storyteller, wrote in *13 Alabama Ghosts and Jeffrey* that Wells had been arrested on "vague circumstantial evidence." Wells shouted, "I am innocent. If you kill me, I am going to haunt you for the rest of your lives!" Windham writes that accounts vary as to whether the lightning bolt or the lynch mob killed the victim but that "everyone agrees that this was the last night of Henry Wells' life."

Windham's book helped to popularize the legend, and now tourists frequently stop in Carrollton to view the image. A large arrow points to the correct pane in the courthouse garret, and for a few coins you can look at the face through a telescope positioned across the street. A historical marker tells a short version of the ghost story.

What appears to be a man's face stares from the indicated pane on the courthouse's north side. (Photo by Brandon Pierce)

The rescue of the courthouse itself provides a modern chapter to the story. By 1999, the building's paint was cracking and its roof needed substantial repairs. There was even talk of tearing down the building. Court proceedings already had moved across the street to a new building.

Nora Johnson, a life-long resident of Pickens County, joined with six other women from the town to prevent the demolition. "Us ladies said, 'You are going to tear it down over our dead bodies,'" she said. The women formed the Pickens County Courthouse Preservation Society to raise money for the needed repairs.

"Everyone got out and begged money," she said. The society raised $2,000 in private donations and $100,000 from state grants.

"We just got in there and did it," she said. The society continues to raise money by holding a 5K run every year on Halloween. The group also sells mugs for $8. The mugs have a drawing of the courthouse on one side and a four-paned window on the other. When you put hot liquids in the mug, a face appears on the lower-right pane.

The society has put the funds to work, and the exterior renovations are finished. During the project, some of the workers worried that the window pane could be broken. They put a piece of plywood over the glass to protect it. Later, when Johnson inspected their progress, one of the workers said, "We put your picture on there." The men had painted a face on the wooden board.

The men might not have worried about the glass had known the rest of the story. In 1928 a powerful hailstorm hit Carrollton. Martha Leatherwood, 89, lived near the town at the time. She was spending the night with a group of girls at her friend's house, and the children huddled together waiting for the storm to pass. The next morning they headed to town and ice was still on the ground.

When Leatherwood and her friends reached the courthouse, they saw what would eventually become part of the ghost story. Hail had broken every window on the north side of the courthouse except one -- the one with the ghostly image etched on it.

A newspaper account confirms the severity of the storm. "All windows on the north and west sides of buildings, unless protected, were shattered," the paper reports. "Hail stones fell that measured fourteen inches in circumference, and they were formed something like a sweet

gum burr, covered with points on every side."

A popular variation on the story holds that the window has been broken several times and that each time the image has returned. The image has been scrubbed with soap and gasoline, said Johnson, but it is the same window.

People often tell her they know for a fact that the window has been replaced, and Johnson has learned to keep her mouth shut.

"You don't disagree with anybody's tales that they have heard," she said.

John Carmichael contributes to *Dateline Pickens*. He earned his master's degree in journalism in May 2002 from the University of Alabama.

## ANOTHER FACE IN COURTHOUSE ATTIC WINDOW

Mystery Face in Courthouse Window Now Has Company
In Another Face on New Pane Just Replaced.

The story of the Courthouse face is one familiar to all the inhabitants of Pickens County, and its fame has spread abroad. Many strangers coming to Carrollton make inquiry about the fact, and many have come from a distance merely to see for themselves the reputed picture in a window pane that cannot be seen except from certain angles. None have ever gone away doubting its presence. The picture is there. In order to get the best view of it, one has to stand directly in front of the Courthouse and look up at the window, for it is in the attic window just below the cornice. The features of a man in severe pain stares one right in the face as one gazes upon it.

Many explanations have been given for its presence and many are the stories that have been told about is mysterious appearance. The window has been examined by dozens of people and none have been able to see anything on the glass either the inside or the outside of the window. It is a plain ordinary window pane.

On December 30th, 1927, a dreadful hailstorm shattered windows and demolished roofs of the houses in Carrollton, and among the windows broken in the courthouse was this small gable window in the attic in which the mysterious picture appears. One pane in this window was shattered, but the picture remained unharmed and still stares one in the face. Visitors from other sections of the county came to Carrollton the following day to view the

now wrecked village, and expressed astonishment when they found that the picture remained while the other panes were broken. Several men requested that a mechanic be set up to screen the window in order to preserve the picture.

The weather remained so cold that no effort was made to repair the broken windows till Thursday, January 5th, when a careful carpenter was selected to go to the attic and repair the window. He was given very positive instructions not to break or damage the pane containing the picture. Judge Robison went so far as to tell him he would receive no pay for any of this work if he broke the pane containing the picture. This carpenter was J.E. Oglesby, a well known farmer in the county, who follows the carpenter's trade out of farm season, and is man of good reputation. He went to the attic, measured the space for the broken panes and went to a nearby hardware store and had the manager cut the glass for him. When they were cut he climbed again to the courthouse attic and fitted them into the window. When the job was done, Judge Robison was called to see that it was properly done. The Judge looked, rubbed his eyes and look again, then he said, "Oglesby, how come that face on the pane just replaced." Oglesby looked, and there, plainly stared another face from the pane just replaced, and still the ghastly faces looked down on the crowd that quickly assembled.

The onlookers were accusing in their remarks to the Judge and the carpenter, but they denied all responsibility, and then the hardware man was blamed, but he too, denied having anything to do with it. While they argued, the picture disappeared, and the late arrivals said there was nothing to it, and started back to their

there it is again, and when the crowd lifted their eyes to the window there stared again the new face plain as a photograph on the new window pane. It comes and goes as one watches it. It's there and isn't there in the short time of five seconds.

A minister and a layman were standing looking at it, when the parson said, "Look, it is going away," and the layman exclaimed, "Damned if it aint."

Oglesby said he is not superstitious, but that picture has disturbed him even in his hours he sleep. He dreamed Saturday night that some one came to his bed in the darkness of the night and told him not to discuss the picture when asked about it, that it appeared for a purpose and that the people of Carrollton would some day know and understand its meaning, and until then, it would not be wise to discuss it. Since then Oglesby has positively refused to discuss it.

In 1876 the county courthouse at Carrollton was burned with all its contents, and the story goes that two negroes, George Wells and Sam Burkhalter, were arrested and charged with the burning, that Wells was shot in making the arrest and died in the county jail, and that Burkhalter was tried and found guilty and sentenced to be hanged. He lay in jail a long time and his hair grew to be very long and shaggy. He was hanged at the appointed time with his shaggy hair clustered about his troubled face. The first picture is said to be a perfect likeness of him and stares right into ones eyes with his horrible trouble look. The new picture is said to resemble Lee Summerville, a negro who killed Deputy Bert C. Johnson, a little more than a year ago, and who made his escape and has not yet been apprehended, though a negro answering his description was recently slain by a Sumter County deputy in York, Ala.

A colored minister stood looking at the picture a few days ago and was asked by the Probate Judge to explain it. He said: "I am unable to interpret it, but it evidently means something," and he warned the people of his congregation not to speak slightly of it, for it might bring them untold sorrow.

Whether the stories are all true or not, the pictures are there, and hundreds of people come each day to look on them and as many explanations are given for the cause of their appearance, but none can deny they are there, and that the new one comes and goes as one looks at it.

A travelling man stopped in the little village only a few days ago and the first sight he asked to "see" was the face in the window. It was shown him and he looked at it for a moment and then said. "I'll bet a hundred dollars that negro was innocent."

### WON'T COME OFF

The offending pane has been removed and carefully examined by responsible men of the village. J.E. Oglesby, S.S. Pearson, County Sheriff E.L. May and W.A. McCain, pastor of the Baptist Church and like the other pane no face was visible at a close view. The pane was thoroughly washed with acid. Then the group returned to the street where a crowd had gathered. Both faces were still there, but a return to the attic and a close view from behind revealed no pictures. There they are however, one troubled and in pain, the other bold and defiant for all Carrollton to see. The skeptics shrugged and dropped the charges preferred against the carpenter, who has been known here for many years as an honest man.

■ Siegelman gives up idea of working by fire at his office. 3B

## Committee seeks money to preserve 'Face in Window'

### By TOMMY STEVENSON
Executive Editor

CARROLLTON — Frightened and horrified, Henry Wells must have been terrified at what he saw when he looked down from the third-floor garret of the new Pickens County Courthouse, where he was being held prisoner in early February 1878.

Gathered on the north side of the courthouse square that cold and stormy night was a mob that had come for him, because he was accused of a...

As Henry Wells pressed his face to the pane in the lower right corner of the window, a bolt of lightning illuminated the horrific scene below him. In that instant Wells' terrified visage was etched into the window much as a flash of light etches itself into conventional photographic film.

*The photograph shows the face of Henry Wells in the window of the Pickens County Courthouse in Carrollton.*

*Larry Green, 10, looks up through a telescopic viewer at The "Face in the Courthouse Window" at the Pickens County Courthouse.*

Please see FACE Page 4B

Henry Wells

# PART TWO

# BOOK

As we walked one dreary evening, while keeping up with the latest updates on the April 27 tornado, I felt that it was going to happen. Around five that day, the weather began to change. Tornado warnings began to go off. I knew this was the big one. My daughter and her friend wasn't paying any attention to the news. I then heard the weatherman saying it is coming toward the university mall. I then told everyone to get in the bathroom. My daughter was laughing, saying, "Momma doing us like they do us in school," thinking it was just a routine. My husband said no, to just get in the hallway. I then said, "Seriously, no. Everybody, get in the bathroom." I went into my bedroom and anointed myself with oil, told my daughter to get in the bathtub, and held my grandbaby in my arms firmly in a blanket, telling my daughter, "Now when I give Jocguel, my *grandson*, to you. *You* hold him firmly and don't let go," and then I began to pray, asking God to please save us.

At this time, I was feeling calm and not afraid. I was ready. By this time, the house began to shake, and we could hear the roaring of the tornado as it approached us. It got louder and louder and felt as though the house was getting ready to be blown away. My daughter began to scream out my name, saying momma. I told her to pray. Her friend, who was sitting on the top of the stool, dropped his head and began to pray also. They knew now that this was it. No one can stop it. Lights were out by now. With a candle lit, it was real, then everything got quiet. My husband reached to open the bathroom door. I told him no, it's not over. By this time, the house started to shake again and the roaring was even louder. I felt like the house was getting ready to blow away. We all were praying, then it finally stopped. It seemed as though it lasted an hour.

We came out of the bathroom and looked outside. Trees were all over. Strong winds had blown dirt and shingles from the roofs under the doors. We looked out back. My pecan tree was blown down into the neighbor's yard from the root that sit to the side of the shed in the backyard. It fell in the neighbor's yard on the right, and a tree fell into my yard from the left. My shed was still standing, and everyone else's shed around me was blown down When we got to the front of the house, a lady walked up and said to me, "A little girl is hurt. She needs your help. Her head is bleeding" I heard her, but then I can't hear her because my daughter is screaming loud and crying, calling me and saying momma after she seen the disaster. Out to the left and in the back of me was damaged, blown down, or blown away.

I knew I had to stay calm. I'm trying to calm my daughter down. She was thinking that all her friends that she goes to school with were hurt, and just the devastation alone was too much for everyone. I don't know how much time it took before the lady walked up to the edge of my driveway and told me again, "A little girl needs your help, and she is bleeding from her head." As I looked at her, I was saying to myself, why didn't she just help the girl? I knew then I had to get my focus on what to do, so I immediately ran in the house and got a big towel, and I wet it with cold water, went to the car that they were sitting in. I asked who has a head injury. She answered me, "The little girl, her mother, sister, and two brothers was in there." I could not see anything but their eyes. They were covered in debris and dirt. After I got her head tied up, I said out loud that she needed to get to the hospital right away, and trucks began to come out of nowhere, breaking the limbs on the trees lying across the streets. I looked up, and the lady that came and got me came across the railroad track in a blue car, tore about down to the ground, pulled up, looked at me, and said, "I'll take her to the hospital but there was no way out." The trucks did not give up. They kept going back and forward until the limbs were broken up enough so the car could get through. I didn't understand how the car went through all that debris. After she pulled off with the little girl, the siren went off again. They say another tornado is on the way. I asked the little girl's mother in the broken-down car that was just sitting there in the street in front of my neighbor's house on the left if they needed help because they were just sitting there in that car that wasn't going anywhere. I asked them if they needed help and she said yes. They did not have family here, and she asked me if they could come to my house. I said yes and helped the mother get to my house. She had a big gash out of her left outer ankle. We had to hurry to get inside.

My Daughter Chassade

My Grandson Jocquel

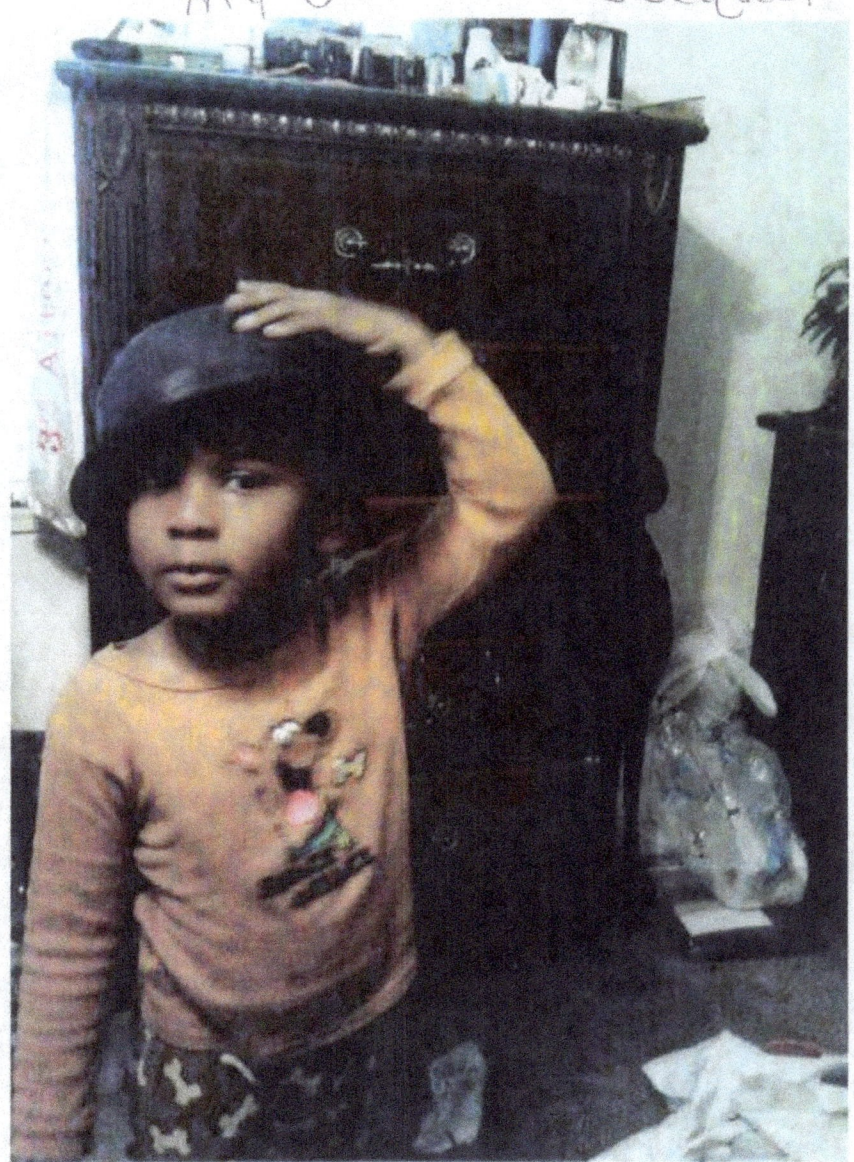

# TORNADO

As we walked up my driveway, the siren went off. I looked back and saw people from all races walking down the street. Some had dirt, some had blood all over their bodies, looking straight ahead, looking as though they had nowhere to go or didn't know what to do. Most of them was in a daze. People started to ask me if they could stay at my house until the storm passed. I said yes. I even saw a family, my husband's family. I had my car porch full of people, house full of people. I've never seen a disaster like this one before. It was like unbelievable but for real. People was saying all kinds of things, like I got to get out of here Some were cussing, and some were just plain outright scared to death. As I looked around, I couldn't see how I was going to get all these people in the house. I had the children sitting on the floor and the adults all around them. Everyone was in the house now. I went outside to look, and I knew the storm was just about here. I told everyone to stop talking. It is here.

I began to pray out loud. "Lord, protect us." The wind picked up. It was so hot in the house by now, no power on, so I opened the back door so the wind could cool everyone off. I stood outside, facing the back door that was opened, put my hands in the air to the Lord, prayed out loud so everyone who could hear me to try and take some of the fear away. I saw on everyone's face as they were looking at one another like this is it. I then went inside the house and closed the door, and the roaring of the wind picked up. The rain was heavy. I kept praying. It soon went over us. People began to leave, walking out of this area, trying to get to their families and friends. Some had nowhere to go.

The family of five that I had helped wasn't from here. They moved here from another city and had nowhere to go. The mother asked me if they could stay here because they didn't have family here and had nowhere to go. I said yes. Some stayed until the rescue workers came through and told them about shelters they could go to, so as the evening went on, we couldn't see inside the house or outside. I lit candles all over the house so we could see. The little boy kept scream-ing when his older brother tried to pick him up, so with my having a nursing experience, I asked the mother if it would be okay if I looked at her four-year old's bottom to see what was hurting him. She said yes. I got the flashlight and looked, and he had a big cut on his bottom. It was wide open but not bleeding. It had clogged itself. I knew he had to get to the hospital right away because he had a fever setting in and had started to sleep a lot. I then began to look at everybody's arms and legs to see who was hurt. The mother had a big gash out of her ankle. Her other son had a small cut on the back of his calve. The younger girl around ten looked fine. I asked her if she was okay and she said yes.

I then dialed 911, but no one could get up in here at the time, but they are working fast as they can to get to my house. The streets were blocked by trees and debris. By now, the four-year-old boy was sleeping too much, and his breath-ing was shallow. I didn't want to scare the mother, so I told his seventeen-yearold brother to wake him up and don't let him go back to sleep. Someone was coming to get him and his mother soon. I began to pray to myself, asking God to please send someone. I walked to the end of the driveway and saw a police officer from Northport, Alabama, a lady officer. I did not see a police car. She asked me if I need help. I told her, "I do. I have two people inside that need to get to the hospital right away." By this time, the mother had a fever setting in. It was time to go, but I didn't see a vehicle anywhere, just the officer at the time. I was looking around at the damage around me. A big tan truck pulled up. How? I don't know, but it pulled up, and the officer stopped the man in the truck. "Could you take them to the hospital?" she asked him. I looked at the dark-skinned man and he said yes. The officer and I helped the mother and the four-year-old in the truck, and he took off with them.

I reminded Debra, the mother, to find her daughter, Amber, the one who was bleeding from her head while she is out there, and I told her that Ladereus, her son, and the baby girl could stay here until she get back, not knowing that the baby girl needed to go to the hospital because the next morning, I was outside on the car porch. She came out there where I was and started to talk to me. I asked her why she doesn't want to take a bath. She wouldn't tell me. As I combed her hair out later that day, the dirt and the small pieces of wood in her head was really a lot, so it took me a while to get it out, so when her mother came back from the hospital, Debra says she couldn't find her daughter at the hospital. I asked her if she told the nurse about the lady that took her out there. Debra said the nurse told her that no one came in with her and that she was by herself, so now we are worried about where she was. She was not at the hospital, and we didn't know where she was.

A few days went by, we still haven't heard from Amber. We couldn't drive out and no one could come in except on foot, so we took the barbecue grill and cooked, warmed up water for baths and dishes. A few days later, volunteers were able to come in and bring us water and food because, by now, the water was turning brown, and there was gas leaks around us. The National Guard was walking around, letting us know when to use a lighter and when not to. May I remind you, I am constantly praying that we could find Amber. One morning, I walked out of the side door to the car porch, and I heard someone calling my name Brenda Turner. As the voice got closer, I began to yell out, "I am Brenda Turner." As I got to the edge ofthe driveway, I looked down the street and saw two volunteers running my way, and when they got to me, they said they have been looking for me because they have a little girl named Amber at one of the shelters in the area, and she didn't know my address but remembered my name, and they said I didn't know where her family was. I said they are here at my house. They started jumping up and down with joy, saying, "Yaya, we have really been looking for you."

So Amber was reunited with her family. And everything was lining up, but I still felt that something else was wrong because the baby girl still had not taken a bath, so I'm thinking, *Please tell me why she won't take a bath.* She then asked me to come outside on the car porch with her. That's where we hung out because we didn't have power for air conditioner and TV. We did have a radio. The real TV was outside, watching what was going on and watching the church members from a church in Northport cut the trees up in my yard and setting up a place in my front yard so people can get food and water in the neighborhood and bring medical kits to me so I could help the family change their bandage. All of them were hurt because when the baby girl, Ta, and I were on the car porch, she came out and pulled up her pants' leg, and she had a big gash out of her thigh. It was wide open, and it was clotted and it looked like the cut I got when I was four years old when I accidentally went through Riverside

High School's window. I showed her the scar on my thigh to help take some of the fear away from her and told her not to worry, that she will be okay like I was.

By this time, we were able to drive in and out, so I went around the corner to Crimson Urgent Care, and they were closed. So I then got someone to take her to the hospital, and at this time, I'm looking at the cut, and it was not bleeding, just deep to the bone like mine was. I told her my story. She wasn't worried any more. All went well. They all have been seen about, but Debra's ankle was hard to heal. She had to keep her foot propped up to keep from getting blood clots, and all of them had to keep their bandage changed every day. Once I got everybody taken care of, it then sunk in that I had nine people in the house and we all were taking this tragedy mentally, physically, and all of the above. They continued to stay in my home for about three weeks until Femur gave them finances to get a hotel until their house was ready.

During all this, I could see Jesus's face shaped in the trees all around me. I even could see his face in the debris of the broken trees on the side of the road, in the yard across the street, looking toward Alberta City it was lit up from the big light that the National Guard had sitting there, before you go across the tracks to Alberta City coming from an army tank that was keeping looters out. There was a broken tree across the street next door to that house, and I could see Jesus face in the tree. One night, we were sitting on the porch. The kids were playing cards with my daughter Chassade, and *Jay* said, "I am scared." I ask him why and he said, "I see a face looking at me in that tree." Then I knew that I was not losing it. I told him that it was Jesus, and he got okay. Two doors down from me, I had seen Jesus in a tree in their yard from my backyard. It is as though he has thrones on his head, and by the way, we can still see it from my backyard during the spring when the leaves are on the trees.

Some people can see it, some can't.

Before the storm, I had seen a man on Loop Road here in Tuscaloosa. He was just standing there with a satchel across both of his shoulders, and as I drove down the road, I looked back and the man had disappeared. I called my mother right away on my cell phone and told her what I had seen. I felt that it was an angel, and this happened right after a storm came through Tuscaloosa and knocked trees down and damaged houses on Loop Road. This was before the April 27, 2011, tornado, but now back to the April 27 tornado, I later found out that the lady that came to get me to help Amber, when she took Amber to the hospital, no one there did not see the lady that took her to the hospital. She never came back to my house, and the nurses at the hospital say they had never seen a lady with blue scrubs on or anybody with Amber when she came into the hospital. Now I'm wondering what happened to the lady-no name, no number, nothing.

So a few months later, as I'm reading the newspaper, I had seen the same lady that came to my house to tell me that a little girl, who was Amber, needed help and that the little girl was bleeding from her head. Now I am sitting here looking at her picture in the newspaper. I said to myself, "There she is," and as I read the write-up about her, it said that she lived in Alberta City and that she was killed in the tornado and that she was a nursing assistant at a nursing home in the Alberta area, and her husband said that she was getting ready to go back to school for an RN. The most amazing thing is that she had on blue scrubs. Tears began to roll down my face while I'm thinking to myself, God had people showing me what I needed to do that was not alive and was a sprit and I encountered that. And that made me happy to know that I did obey. I then called Debra and told her to get the newspaper and what I had seen. I knew something was different about her because when I think back, she did not have any dirt on her, but everyone else that walked out of Alberta City had dirt all over their bodies, but she was clean, and her hair looked like she had just *gotten it* done, and she only said the few words that she said to me. And when I was helping Amber, I looked up and she was coming across the railroad track in a blue car that was torn up from the tornado. But I didn't think at that time how was she driving that car. I couldn't even hear the motor run. I knew then God was using me.

About a week later, after the tornado, I rode around in the area to see the damage, and I see a man walking through the debris out in Alberta City with a cane, looking just like the black man that I see over on Loop Road that disappeared, so I thought when I saw him, how can that old man walk through all that debris? And not only that, the signs says No Trespassing Keep Out. No one was allowed to go out there, so as I looked back just as before on Loop Road, the man had disappeared. I'm saying to myself now, okay, I am tripping, as people say, and feeling chills from head to toe, so I called my mother again. A few weeks later, my daughter Chassade, goddaughter Rachel, and I were backing out of Captain D's parking lot on McFarland Boulevard. And behold, there he stood again, but this time, he was standing in front of my truck, then he walked real slow by the passenger side, did not look up at my daughter Chassade, my foster daughter Rachel, or me. Then I told them, "There goes the angel I've been telling you all about." We looked like, how is this old man going to make it across the street with all this traffic? Like this McFarland Boulevard is the busiest street in Tuscaloosa.

As we backed out and looked, he was already across the highway, walking behind the Raceway gas station. Time had gone by, perhaps several months. Rachel and I were riding downtown Tuscaloosa on Sixth Street one day, and we saw him walking toward the municipal court building, and we got to the stop sign, looked back, and he was gone. Months went by. One night, my daughter and I were riding on Jack Warner Parkway.

We all call it Fifteenth Street, and as we made a left turn at Crimson Urgent Care, Chassade asked me, "Did you see your angel?

I said, "No, why didn't you tell me?"

She said, "I did, Momma."

I told her we were going by the house and pick up her friend and that we were going back because I want to see my angel.

On the way back, Chassade said, "He got on a white robe this time, Momma."

I knew this was meant for me to see. We went back, and there he was, walking down Jack Warner Parkway, walking real slow between Crimson Urgent Care and the Fabric Store, walking with a cane, and he had the same satric across both his shoulders, and it was the same man and he did have on a white robe. We went *around* the block, came around again, and he was gone, and I'm thinking, *There is no way this old man could ever walk that fast or run*, so this confirmed it as far as my angel. I know they watched over us whether we see them or not.

Time has flown by. It is now time for the play that goes on at the Pickens County Courthouse, *The Face in the Courthouse Window*, who was Henry Wells, in April 2013. I missed the one in 2012 because I had to have a procedure done on my breast again. The test showed sign of cancer, they say again, but after all had been done, I did not have cancer. So now I thank God once again for healing me and thankful for all the people that prayed for me. Now this year 2013, I went to the play, and it was even better than the years before with the gospel choir singing those hymns like my family used to sing them back in the day. I had to join in and sing along with them on some songs because it took me back to when I was at Oak Grove Church. But now a few days before I went, I asked God and Henry Wells to show me the answers I am looking for because I still feel that I am missing something and what is it, to please show me.

Lo and behold, I was sitting, talking to my friend about it. I jumped up, went in the house, got Henry Wells's picture, and I also got pictures of my great-grandpa Oscar Wells and his dad, who is my great-great-grandpa, clifford Wells, and I put them down and kept looking at it, saying, "What is it? Come on, help me. What is it?" And then I saw something that shocked my friend when I said, "Look, Papa Cliff." We called him. He had the same features as Henry Wells, including the clothes. Both of them are wearing compatible, even the hat. I'm thinking aloud, saying Henry looks like my great-great-grandpa. Is this my papa Clifford's image in that window? And maybe they told the people that he was dead from a gun shooting in the leg, so they did not hang him. Because from Barry Bradford's findings, his face was etched in the window on January 30, 1878, by lightning and was later arrested in Fairfield and then died from gunshot wound while attempting to flee authorities.

Now this I can believe because I remember Papa Cliff and I believe that someone covered for his life and saved it, and I believe that they changed his name from Henry Wells to Clifford Wells, my great-great-grandfather. I am now going by what I see and what I know I feel that I have found the missing piece. Thank you, Jesus and Almighty God on high, for giving me this insight, something that I believe is the truth. What a mystery. Now I understand myself more and how God works with me because my mother, Laura Hurst Smith, her mother Ora Deal Wells Hurst, her father Oscar Wells, his father Clifford Wells were and are powerful praying people, and it is in me too. Thank you, Lord.

This is my conclusion, while Dora Johnson, president of the Pickens County Courthouse, and Barry Branford have all the evidence of what really happened, the travel channels aired a segment on The Face in the Courthouse Window, and still sticking to the tales that was told long time ago.

I hope, one day, the travel channel will be interested in the truth. As I have learned over the years, never say never. I have seen a lot been through a lot and still, to this day, experienced all kinds of things including having a dream that I see Jesus standing on this earth from the ground up through the clouds, and as I told the dream, I sketched it on paper. I've never seen anything like this before. I'm paying attention to what he is trying to show me. Yes, I can't really say exactly what it is, but with all the things that is going on in this world today, who's to say? During the dream, it looked like I called my mother and asked her, "Do you see it? Do you see Jesus in the sky?" And she said yes. After all this occurred, one day, it stormed, and after the storm, I went outside and looked up because I had never seen the sky so beautiful before. I asked Richard to take a picture of it, and I looked at it. It did not look the same as it does on camera. It looked like little colored cotton balls when you look at it. It was special I then called my mom and asked her where she was. She said she was coming out of church from Bible study. I asked her, "Do you see the sky?" She said yes. It was ironic. I had never seen anything like it. After I hung the phone up, I realize I just did the same thing that I dreamed. God is showing me a lot. Now I accept that I'm going to take one day at a time, even when people treat me wrong or falsely accuse me.

If they lie on me, talk about me, abuse me, it doesn't matter. I know that I know God is sitting on the throne. Jesus walked with me every day, and I will try to do his will the best that I know how and let him lead me. I pray for my strength in the Lord. I've learned that I can't put my trust in no one but God and his son Jesus Christ. Why is it so hard for people to accept the truth even if they see it? I give him all the honor and all the glory. I never tried to put myself before Jesus or God because he has showed me what he can do, and I accept it in the name of Jesus. The Bible says go by what you see and what you hear, and I shall do so I will be obedient.

The
# Face
In The
# Courthouse
# Window
By Barry Bradford

Performed Each April

w.courthousewindow.com

"The strength of t
script and the
will remain
in our memorie

# 'Courthouse' performed this week

By Alexis Paine
Special to Tusk

Friday April 12th 2013 Tuscaloosa News

Jerrell Bowden, right, and Willie Williams rehearse a scene from "The Face in the Courthouse Win Pickens County Courthouse in Carrollton on April 3, 2010. This year's production will be held at 7 p and 7 p.m. Saturday at the Pickens County Courthouse in Carrollton.

**P**eering down from the Pickens County Courthouse, the eerie image of Henry Wells' face permanently plastered on a window pane stares at those who dare to meet its gaze. At least, that is how the legend is told. Actors from the University of West Alabama and community actors will perform "The Face in the Courthouse Window," a play written about the legendary Wells, today and Saturday.

Wells, a freed slave, was accused and convicted of the 1876 burning of the Pickens County Courthouse. As the tale goes, Wells was chased by a mob to a newly erected courthouse on Jan. 30, 1878, in the midst of a storm. He stood on the garret roof, looking down on the people determined to hang him. As Wells was threatening to haunt the mob if they killed him, lightning struck a nearby tree and etched the man's features in the window of the courthouse. Wells was later arrested in Fairfield and died from a gunshot wound obtained while attempting to flee authorities.

The play, written by Barry Bradford, was first performed under the sponsorship of the Pickens County Courthouse Preservation Foundation, in an attempt to save the almost 130-year-old building where Wells' face can still be seen.

Willie Williams, director and actor playing Henry Wells, said the play shows the racism and economic hardship of the post-Civil War South. Williams said these topics are important parts of Alabama history, despite their ugliness.

"A lot of the images and ideas in the script may remind us about things that we might not want to remember," Williams said. "But I think that's important about preserving Alabama history, so we can make strides for a brighter future. I think it's destructive to block out history."

The cast performs shows for school-children before the play opens to the public. Williams said the students are able to learn a lot about history from this production.

"I think (students) gain a larger perspective and insight in how people lived in 1800s Alabama," Williams said. "It gives them a deeper perspective and first-hand knowledge with a story from their town. Some of them have been able to identify with the characters, and I think that's beautiful."

Ashley Betts, the actress playing Wells' wife, Caroline, learned about the face in the courthouse window about two years ago. The native of Toomsuba, Miss., said she has learned a lot about Alabama history from performing in this play and hopes audience members are inspired by the production.

"I hope (the audience) wants to know

## 'THE FACE IN THE COURTHOUSE WINDOW'

**What:** Play based on the historical event.
**When:** 7 p.m. today, 2 and 7 p.m. Saturday.
**Where:** Pickens County Courthouse, Carrollton.
**Cost:** $20.
**More:** www.courthousewindow.com.

great like a moral through what happens through the story of Henry Wells."

Although the play is set in the late 19th century, many of the struggles Wells and other characters encounter are still common today, Williams said. Wells is dealt a poor hand and forced to deal with it the best he can, which should be relatable to audience members, he said.

Betts said she learned about emotions, loyalty and burdens as she connected to her character. A newcomer to the production, Betts had some difficulty falling into line with actors who had played their roles for years, but was able to learn from the seasoned cast.

Many people return to see the play year after year, Williams said. While much of the production remains the

be different than years past. The direc-

All proceeds from

# PLAY

It is April 2013. Time for the play, which starts April 12 at the Pickens County Courthouse. I went on that Saturday. I wasn't going to stay. I was going to just see Miss Johnson, Barry, cast members, and all the wonderful people that were a part of this play.

When I told Ms. Johnson I wasn't staying, she said, "Oh yes, stay. You got to hear the choir."

I said, "Choir? Oh yes."

But I told her I did not purchase a ticket, and she said I got your ticket, and that made me happy that she wanted me to stay. The cellar door was open that goes down to the jail cell where Henry Wells was in. I went down there, nervous at first, but as my friend went down in there, I followed him so I wouldn't be down there by myself. That was before Ms. Johnson got there after I came out. Then I see Ms. Johnson and her granddaughters and their boyfriends coming down the street.

When she got there, she asked me, "Did you get pictures of your grandfather's jail cell for your book?"

I told her yes, and then she introduced me to her granddaughters and their boyfriends as Henry Wells's great-great-granddaughter. It was like she knew I had figured it out that Henry Wells was my great-great-grandfather. I smiled, and we took pictures. The play was even better this time, and as they sing, I sang along with them with the songs that I knew. I cried again. The gospels sounded like the ones my family used to sing, and when the play was over, I had seen other people crying. One lady that worked there told me, "I can never get through the play without crying." I told her I can't either. It was very, very good. Ms. Johnson and our friend from the First National that asked Ms. Johnson to start the play in the beginning were clapping and giving God some praise. Yes, the play is that good, and as I was leaving, I took pictures of all the actors in the play.

Henry Wells Jail Sail

Henry Wells Jail sail

Dora Johnson
Granddaughters & their
Boy Friends

Dora Johnson
&
Brenda Turner

# Cast

HenryWells ..................................................... Willie Williams

Gilliam.................................................Wescott Youngson

Sheriff James Gates...................................... George Thagard

Lem.................................................................David Abston

Mose ...........................................Ligon D Anthony Jackson

Bill Burkhalter........................................ Dequante Shockley

Caroline Wells................................................. Ashley Betts

Monique Brown

E. B................................................................Cody Dixon

John Hunnicut...............................................Justin Barnett

Elliot Moon

Josh Reid

Dr. Sam Hill......................................................... Brad Lang

# ONE SAD RESPONSE

A few months later, they talk about Henry Wells on the travel channel had Barry talk about the truth about Henry Wells, and he told the truth, and they still tried to make it seemed as though he did not know the truth, but they had all the facts and still got the facts at the Carrolton Courthouse. Ms. Johnson was very upset because the travel channel still tried to make it seemed as though Henry Wells was hung by the mob. That's not the truth, so after reading my book, and all the proof is in here, maybe they will want the real truth. One thing I will say about Ms. Johnson, she made sure she gave me all the truth, and Barry put it together through the play. We cannot change the facts.

Early one morning, I was looking at the news after Thanksgiving and before Christmas, saying that Ms. Johnson had passed on.

The tears are rolling. We had become close and I was thinking about the last time I had seen her at the play. I was so glad I stayed, not knowing that was the last time I would see her. I really want to see the truth come out. That is all. She wanted was the real truth to come out about Henry Wells, the face in the courthouse window.

# Fabled face to get TV time

## Travel Channel to air segment on Carrollton legend

Staff report

The Travel Channel's program "Monumental Mysteries" will air a segment tonight about the legend surrounding the face in the courthouse window in Carrollton.

The segment will be on at 8 p.m. on channel 69 for Comcast cable customers.

According to the Travel Channel's website, the program "scours the country for America's most extraordinary monuments and reveals the amazing mysteries hidden within."

The legend surrounding the Pickens County Courthouse begins with Henry Wells, a freed slave.

In 1878, Wells, who was accused

SEE FACE | 3B

## ON THE WEB

■ Have you seen the face in the courthouse window in Carrollton? Vote in our Web poll at www.tuscaloosanews.com.

■ For more on the show, visit www.travelchannel.com/video/ haunting-by-an-executed-slave.

# FACE

CONTINUED FROM PAGE 1B

of burning down the previous courthouse, looked down from the garret room window of the Pickens County Courthouse at a mob threatening to lynch him.

A bolt of lightning struck the window pane and etched what seems to be his features in it, where the image can be seen to this day.

During the Civil War, the original courthouse had been burned to the ground by Union soldiers commanded by General John T. Croxton, who also torched the University of Alabama. In 1878, the replacement building was burned to the ground, and Wells, a freed slave, was convicted of the act. But he wasn't arrested until two years later in Fairfield, south of Aliceville.

Legend has it Wells protested his innocence and threatened to haunt the lynch mob. Then the lightning struck. Wells died of gunshot wounds sustained in his arrest.

"The Face in the Courthouse Window" was featured in Kathryn Tucker Windham's "13 Alabama Ghosts and Jeffrey" book.

Each year, Carrolton hosts a production of the Barry Bradford play "The Face in the Courthouse Window," which is performed inside the courthouse.

# TV show aired about Pickens Co. Courthouse but truth was not told

By Elaine Moody
Gazette Staff

**M**any area residents and people nationwide watched last Thursday night as the Travel Channel on TV aired a segment on the Pickens County Courthouse about their "Face in the Courthouse Window."

This show, having been promoted as a true story about the mysterious face in the window at the courthouse, was a complete disappointment to those who knew the real story.

"We are so disappointed in what they did. They added and put in there what they wanted," said Dora Johnson, who is the President of the Pickens County Courthouse Preservation Foundation.

"It has taken us 14 years to get the truth out about Henry Wells, and they threw us a curve in the back," lamented Johnson.

The truth she is speaking of came to light about 14 years ago.

▶ See **Courthouse** Page 3B

Photo by Elaine Moody

Above, Mrs. Dora Johnson, president of the Pickens County Courthouse Preservation Foundation, says the Travel Channel's show on the "Face in the Window" did not portray truthfully what happened.

At left — The beautiful courthouse located in Carrollton is steeped in legend and visited by tourists year around.

# Courthouse ——— From Page 1

while researching in the courthouse prior to its renovation.

"The Face in the Courthouse Window," a play written by Barry Bradford, has been presented for three years at the courthouse in Carrollton. Bradford, who was featured in the Travel Network's show as moderator for the segment about the courthouse window and prisoner Henry Wells, didn't know they were going to make up the ending, said Johnson.

The segment lasted about 10 minutes and local viewers who had high hopes about the show being seen nationwide and the publicity it would give to Pickens County, were very disappointed, according to Johnson.

Wells, a black man, was not lynched as the TV show portrayed, according to Johnson. "He was shot twice in the leg as he was trying to escape from a lynch mob. One went into the flesh, one went into the bone. Dr. Samuel Hill tried to get the bullets out but could not get the one out of the bone. This was in June. Gangrene set in and Wells died in February the following year."

Johnson said that about 14 years ago, the truth was found in papers, law books and newspapers that were found in the courthouse.

"It's all here. Anyone can come see what we found. I would like people to come read for themselves the truth," urged Johnson.

# TESTIMONIES

My daughter, Brenda Sue Lee Turner, has always had dreams. When she got older, she began to tell me about her dreams, and sometimes her dreams will come true before the end of the day. When she tells you about a dream, you can expect something to come out of it. And when she prays, she doesn't play. She has always helped people. The list is too long. I was a dreamer, and my mother was a dreamer, and Brenda was blessed with special gifts as a baby in my womb.

— Laura Lee Hurst Smith

I don't know where to begin, but I guess this will have to do. It's about my wife, Brenda Turner. I guess you would say she has a gift. She sees things through her dreams. What I mean is that what she dreams usually comes true. She dreamed about the March 27, 2011 tornado. It came true. She has dreamed about a lot of other tornados and floods that have come true. It's not only disasters that she dreams about. I recall her telling me about a dream she had about her son she carried full term, who was stillborn. She told me how he had come to see her. Now I'm thinking is she okay, but as *God* is my witness, I saw with my own eyes little footprints across our kitchen floor. There were no other children around. These are just a few dreams I have witnessed come true.

— Richard Turner

Me and my godmother Brenda Tuner was on Sixth Street, and I saw a man with shackles on his back. I looked back and then he was gone, and it was the same man we had seen on McFarland.

— Rachel Aultman

# FINAL THOUGHTS

No matter what we go through, always know that God has a plan for all of us through faith in Jesus Christ, whether through good or bad, and know that we all have to be held accountable for our own actions. It may seem like a hard and long road to walk, but you can get there and see that he is for real. And do it through faith and prayer, but we got to go through to get too. Must Jesus bear the cross alone? I have been through a lot, but I will never be ashamed or doubt. I have the confirmation of the Lord, and that's all we need. Life is not a competition but about righteousness and the truth.

# ABOUT THE AUTHOR

Brenda Turner is the former owner of Brenda's Hometown Deli of Tuscaloosa. She graduated from Draughons College and attended Shelton State Community College of Tuscaloosa, Alabama. Brenda worked as a medical assistant in Atlanta, Georgia, and she is currently a proud mother and grandmother.

www.ingramcontent.com/pod-product-compliance
Lightning Source LLC
Chambersburg PA
CBHW060538130626
46553CB00002B/817